medianus

Human money for a mature world

Walter Panhuber

Copyright © 2014 Walter Panhuber
All rights reserved

www.medianus.at
Author: Walter Panhuber
Proofreading: Annette Guerin

ISBN-13: 1496194004
ISBN-10: 978-1496194008

Content

			Prolog	6
1			**Politics**	8
	1		Tradition	8
	2		Pyramid of power	12
	3		Corruption	13
	4		Constitution	16
	5		Branches of government	17
		1	Legislature	19
		2	Executive	20
		3	Judiciary	22
		4	Monetative	22
		5	Representatives	24
		6	Summary	25
	6		Austria	26
	7		Secret services	28
	8		Data Security	31
		1	Informer	32
	9		Immigration	34
	10		Development aid	36
2			**Economy**	38
	1		Distribution of assets	39
	2		Money	41
	3		GDP	44
	4		Interest	46
	5		Save Money	51
	6		Taxes	54
		1	Inheritance taxes	55
		2	Income Tax	56
		3	Value Added Tax	62
	7		Social Share Company	63
		1	Election of the Supervisory Board	66
		2	Election process	66
		3	Meeting of the Supervisory Board	70

		4	SSC with the public interest	71
		5	SSC - Exchange	72
		6	Effects by SSC	74
	8		Insurance	74
	9		Subcontracted labor	76
	10		Pension system	78
	11		Unemployment	81
	12		Investment	83
3			**Humane Money**	87
	1		Median	90
	2		Base period	90
	3		Human value	91
	4		Money supply	92
	5		Prime rate	94
	6		State interest	95
	7		Base purchasing power	96
	8		Social system	99
	9		Basket of goods	100
	10		Central bank	101
	11		Trade balance and foreign exchange	103
	12		Paper money and coins	104
	13		The conversion	105
	14		Differences and similarities	114
	15		Summary	116
4			**General thoughts**	120
	1		Compulsory school attendance	120
	2		School system	121
	3		Television	124
	4		Health	125
		1	Vaccinations	126
		2	Aluminum	127
		3	Plastics	133
		4	Teflon	134
	5		Leisure	135

		1 Cabaret and comedy	135
	6	Nuclear energy	137
	7	Energy transition	139
	8	Slavery	140
5		**Philosophical thoughts**	142

Prolog

This book is intended as a working basis for politicians and political parties. It is a call to all responsible citizens of the earth.

1. Unchain your country from the embrace of the multinationals companies.

2. If the primacy of politics restored.

3. Establishes a fair and social market economy.

All the tools you need to find her in this book.

There isn't any party in your country, which has a suitable program, establishes a.

Additional graphics can be found on www.medianus.at. There you can publish your own ideas and comments.

The core point of this book is the "Human money." This new money system includes a reform of the social security and tax system with a. In addition, a reform of administrative, constitutional and business is addressed.

The primate of the politics produces in the long term the human money again and it leads to a revival of the „social market economy".

1. Politics

My greatest wish would be international standards which determine the framework for political action. In addition, a UN that monitor these standards and encroache,if a country leaves the frame.

Unfortunately, there are no such standards, even a UN with the power for such action. Hopefully it does not have to come back to a world war, so that a long overdue reform of the UN is performed.

2. Tradition

Maybe it surprises some, why the subject Tradition is lined up in the column politics at so prominent place. For me is the tradition of the current political, state of the present.

The culture of humanity, or any part thereof, is formed by different ancient traditions. The language of a people is the most important part of the area.

Policy can not be anything else than working on its growing tradition.

Essentially always fight the traditionalists against reformers. The reformers have made it increasingly difficult, because the tradition is a power for themselves.

They can only be changed with considerable resistance, even if the majority of benefits can be expected from the reform.

The reason for this is an emotional matter, the majority trusts in doubt what is already known.

Very few people make the effort, the reason for a reform truly study, they leave it to the elected politicians, it is called also representative democracy.

Usually this fact is exploited shamelessly by the traditionalists. Most satisfies a slight stirring up fears, often with arguments that touch the reform in no way, already there is a suspicious majority for the traditionalists.

My point is it to investigate the reason for this in more detail.

I compare a people with a person, as is the culture of the people of his own behaviour; its traditions are the intellectual superstructure.

There is a spirit in this people, who are all aware and familiar, like the mind of just one family.

Like a person, determined in a referendum the Spirit reveals the current state of the whole, the difference lies in the awareness that tradition is all fully conscious and aware.

You have to change the mind so always first, everything else always results by itself. The advertising industry knows this for a long time.

Another thought relates to the mind, or the spirit, her self-made man-spirit is an institution of the marriage of one establishment to a religious community, known among lawyers as a legal entity.

So there are plethoras of spirits, all of which have relationships to each other. Similarly, there are hierarchies, just like individuals.

Corporations are institutions that operate worldwide.

Allows a nation of such an institution, and thus exert their spirit, power, so it is up to the policy to control such spirits.

If they fail not, so it's only a matter of time until such spirits dominate over the people and their own culture, and thus the tradition degenerates into formal envelope.

1.2. Pyramid of power

Apart from democratic ideas there is a real distribution of power on the planet.

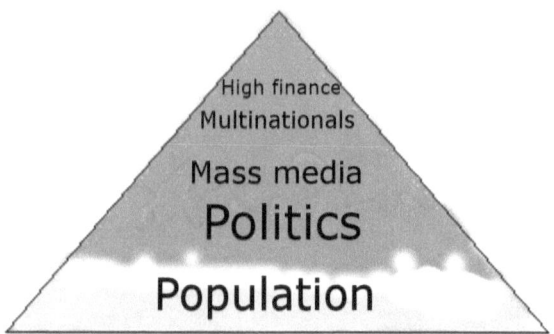

While in past times, the high nobility and the church formed the very top; has clearly established in today's time the high finance at the top.

Identify the natural persons in this power tip turns out to be difficult. While there are individuals and families in this tip, but this disguise their pecuniary circumstances. Above all, there are institutional mights that act today. The exploration of the property situation of these institutes is only possible to a limited range. Level only to the extent, as far as the actual power owner regard this as appropriate.

Under this top is the power structure of the global mass media. These are of course in the main in the possession of high finance.

The belief system of the masses to control ensures the long term power. Alone by the medium of television the majority of the population can be steered today. High finance has arbitrarily high amounts of money and its disposal to buy control of the worldwide television channels. Alternatively provides continuous control of the dependence of advertising revenue.

The politics and the politicians need the mass media to be perceived. Only with a certain fame a politician can hope for the sufficient votes for the desired position. He is fully dependent on the power of the media.

1.3 Corruption

The corruption is the great scourge of human civilization. It is illegal in all states and is often pursued.

However, there is a legal form of corruption, lobbyism. In modern democracies this takes the form of corruption to increase. This worrying development transforms our civilization over the long term in an inhuman society. The policy is increasingly becoming a facade. If you look behind this facade, one finds a people despising system, an ugly face of violence and avance

The mature citizen must absolutely be able to look behind this facade. Only in this way we can counteract this development. Therefore one must understand the functioning of lobbyism.

The easiest way the relationships are to be understood by an example. Here an example from Austria.

The Austrian Federal Chancellor ‚Wolfgang Schüssel, acquired a few years ago some fighter planes for the military. He did not choose the most favorable provider, but supported the corporate interests of the company EADS.

He did not act in the interests of citizens who had given him their democratic voice, but followed other instructions. After completing his capacity as Chancellor, he received a voice in the board of a large German energy group.

The allowance for this post is supposed to be higher than the salary of the Austrian Chancellor.

This process was not illegal. There is no evidence that there are connections between his role as Supervisory Board and his role as chancellor.

The situation is similar with the former German Chancellor Gerhard Schröder. He received after the end of function a voice on the board of Gazprom.

These examples are intended to show how modern lobbyism works. There are no criminal consequences for public officials who act in this manner. It may also be that the both men reach because of their qualifications in the pleisure of heigh compensations

Lobbyism takes place not only in politics. Also, journalists, scientists, doctors, government officials,sportsmen and celebrities are promoted through lobbying if they support the desired interests.

There still exists the page of lobbyism; this is even worse than the first page. The system of lobbyism also eliminates incorruptible critic. Mercilessly persons are pursued and removed if they damage to the system.

For this persecution to apply various means. The innocent is the denigration. For this was especially the word "conspiracy theorists" created. With this taboo word, one tries to make such unplausible people. They are degraded and revealed to the absurdity.

A slightly harder means is the insinuation. This is done using reports in the media in which the person behaviour patterns are subordinated which damage to the respect..

In accordance with the requirements of the funds are ever harder, one does not scare even back before assassinations. Financial resources are available for this purpose in unlimited amounts.

Ultimately, however, always act people in the institutions. They use their networks with people whom they trust, because trust is the basis for lobbyism

1.4. Constitution

Under the Constitution is understood in the policy, the fundamental laws, which, as a rule, can only be changed by a two-thirds majority in Parliament. The Constitution defines the basic political framework of the state. In addition, the fundamental rights defined in the Constitution.

Which emerged from the humanism human rights play in most constitutions, although a role, but of a common standard, the international community is far away. Here it is unfortunately not succeeded in the UN Charter to establish such minimum standards.

Should one day the UN succeed to reform, including such a standard should be set, which then comes into play when a dictatorship collapses. Today Libya would be a good example for their use.

1.5. Branches of government
The ordinary separation of the different branches of government is the biggest weakness of today's democracies. This is due to the strong reference to the democracy of the British Empire.

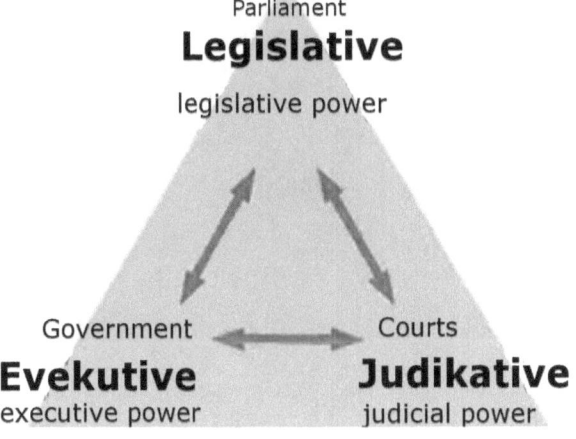

This unnecessary role model should be urgently reconsidered. The constitutions of modern democracies should pay much more to the separation of powers, as to the historical model. One needs neither a plurality of chambers in the legislature still need a replacement for the monarch, the president may be exercised by the President of Parliament without further notice.

The most harmful confusion happens worldwide between legislative and executive branches. However, there are also impermissible influences of the executive in the judiciary. The choice of the government by the Parliament is the largest violation of the separation of powers. The Office of the Chancellor, as the supreme Lord of the executive branch is the most expendable position. A true democracy needs no such positions of power.

Lately, we hear more and more of a fourth state power, the Monetative. I think this also appropriate, provided there is this violence long ago, it is called central bank. I would also like the term Monetative better, along with a democratic reform of central banking.

The following articles show a reform of the state authorities, which should be carried out with the introduction of the Human money.

1.4.1. Legislature

The chief executive officer of the legislature, the office of President of Parliament. He should be elected directly by the people and exercise the office of President. He is the president of the state and also the representative of the nation. A Minister who represents about the party, both legislative and executive branches is not necessary, or even harmful to democracy.

Parliament need only one chamber and is elected directly by the people on the parties. The current party democracy in Austria is quite satisfactory in terms of the legislature.

Also, the controlling body of the Parliament, the Court of Auditors, is very good, he controlled all branches of government, and reports to Parliament, which can then carry out improvements.

Absolutely necessary but further control means, it comes before everything else to the media and the health sector. Truly independent media would be needed as the basis for a true democracy first. However, the corrupt behavior in the health care industry needs an effective control. It's not about financial control, but about relationships with industry, the favors, which are necessary to enter into certain positions.

The choice of a government by the legislature will be abolished. This operation is only a shift in the work of Parliament on this selected group of people. The Parliament itself is on the voting apparatus for this group of people, from ministers, secretaries of state and chancellor, degraded.

Without exception, an employee of another state power may apply for candidacy for any office of the members of the legislature.

1.4.2 Executive

The executive branch includes the Interior Ministry, the Ministry of Foreign Affairs, defense, infrastructure, education department, science, research and the environment.

The very top positions of the ministries are representative elected by the people, but not by the legislature.

For this, all districts in the country to be divided into 10 constituencies, each constituency elects one representative. That candidate with the most supporters becomes the representative of the constituency. Every citizen may at any time change its candidate via the Internet when he learned another candidate know. This choice, which is thus constantly.

If 30% of these representatives have changed, a new election of the Executive peaks is performed. After five years in office, but it is carried out without change of Representatives. This election by 950 representatives caused negligible and done with little effort.

The representatives should have an appropriate education for a senior position in the executive branch. Often, the job of the representatives of the entry into the professional career in the executive will represent. Mandatory However, the qualification is by no means, it is solely responsible for the voters to assess this. Every citizen of a constituency can be theoretically elected representatives.

In the end, the people choose the most popular representatives of the executive leadership of their own. This system creates real expertise in the management of the state in optimal proximity to the people.

Representatives may not be employed in the area of another state power. For example, a lawyer must be Attorney, but not a prosecutor. As a prosecutor, he can only apply to the representatives of the judiciary.

1.4.3. Judiciary

The judiciary comprises the entire judiciary, even the Department of Justice.

The choice of the top positions in the same way as envisioned under the executive. There, too, there is an Internet portal for each constituency in which candidates apply for the post of Representatives. All voters can change their representatives at any time. This also happens on this Internet portal.

Also in the judiciary choose the representatives of the constituencies every 5 years, the peak positions of the judiciary.

However, if people have exchanged in the constituencies more than 30% of the number of representatives will be immediately re-elected. This is performed within 1 week.

The representatives should have a law degree.

1.4.4. Monetative

The Monetative comprises the central bank, the finance department, economic and social.

The Monetative is a swap of sensitive areas from the executive. Therefore, these state power is exclusively in the context of, adopted by the legislature, laws. It is beyond the influence of direct state power (police, military) by outsourcing.

On the other hand, economic influences in the environment and education are avoided.

Be selected the top items in the Monetative in the same manner as already described under executive. In the 95 Austrian districts of 10 representatives are elected by the people. These 950 persons select at least every 5 years, the tips of Monetative.

Candidates for representatives should have training or skills in the fields of economics and finance, tax law, social science and the like.

After the introduction of the Human money the central bank is a political institution, like any other. There is then no lonely arbitrariness by a Fed chairman, as this is handled so often today.

1.4.5. Representatives

With this new system, there are 2850 representatives with expertise, thirty in each political district. Although they have no official authority, they have the connection to the people. Their power will therefore not be negligible, because in her hand is the further fate of ministers in their offices. However, they can be replaced overnight by the people.

In practice, the representatives will of course also belong to different political camps and parties, which the parties have an influence in the government. However, it is impossible for the parties to change the government in the wake of parliamentary elections. Or vice versa. Elections in the executive, judicial and Monetative have no influence on the work of the Parliament.

The function of the representative should not be a professional, so would be a voluntary activity with allowance for the right pay. The representatives are mostly young professionals with training in senior levels of government or. They are either busy in their state power, or aspire to a career there.

1.4.6. Summary

This new Constitution divides the state apparatus in 4 powers. The legislative, judicial, executive and Monetative.

The legislative branch is elected directly by the people on political parties; the President of Parliament is also chosen by the people and is also president of the state. Parliament has only one chamber.

In the other three branches of government is elected representative.

A chancellor or vice chancellor no longer exists. The government form the Minister of individual ministries.

Chosen is the leadership of the ministries of 950 representatives of the constituencies of the state. These elections are held every 5 years.

However, changing 30% of the number of representatives in a state power, the election is carried out within 1 week.

The 2850 own representatives are elected by the people. This election will take place constantly. Every citizen may at any time change the representatives of a government authority.

Overall, the new system will significantly strengthen parliament. Especially in the question and answer sessions, in which the minister to answer questions must be. Or committees of inquiry grievances are revealed much faster than before because of the support in parliament is less.

Then the question of confidence, however, no longer arises, because Parliament is no longer competent. The public pressure, at a misconduct of a minister is, however, immediately sweep away enough of Representatives, so it comes instantly to new elections in the relevant state power. Perhaps the representatives should also have the possibility to decide on a new election.

New laws are usually developed in the future by the ministries, these designs are not easy to get so far by the legislature, as is currently the case.

1.6. Austria

Since Austria joined the European Union, reforms of the political structures are overdue.

We know this for years, but it always fails at the implementation. Even politicians are for reform, but only if they are not personally affected. This policy setting leads to a shift of the necessary reforms in an ever new future.

One therefore needs a roadmap, which provides about 20 years for the completion of the reform. With first steps, however, should be started immediately.

After about 10 years of reform, the reform of the lowest level should be completed. The small structures of the communities have no political function more.

You need to merge no communities. All communities remain. Just like the old villages have remained as political power was handed over to a more central community. Culturally, there are the villages, just like in the future communities.

District councils in rural areas are then selected functions. The skills of communities are all moved to the district. This also applies to any property, as well as organizations and institutions with all employees. Not necessary structures to be sold or closed. Former municipal offices are, as required, used by the district level on. Also, district councils may well take advantage of decentralized offices.

Competencies from the country migrate in the districts according to subsidiary principles.

At the end of 20 years, all remaining powers of the provinces have migrated to the federal ministries. The cultural property of the country remains. The political levels are then the 95 districts and the state. Former mayor found as district councils or district board again. Former country peaks are found together in Parliament.

The long period seems to me to be necessary because there are plenty of jobs to reduce by officials, this requires long transition periods.

1.7. Secret Services

Whether it is legitimate democracies operate secret? We need this question we currently do not face because we live in a world in which such institutions in many areas already have taken power.

Specifically, the United States has strengthened since September 11, 2001 its secret services in a way that conjures up an image of a third world war in secret.

It began with the founding of the FBI at the time of the Russian October Revolution. They had panic in the United States fear that the communist idea would spread to their country. The Federal Bureau of Investigation was established by the Minister of Justice, it was directly in. His task was initially a pure secret service. Man made Communists locate in the country, referred them, if possible, of the country, brought them into prison or killed them.

The longtime head of this institution was J. Edgar Hoover. He was actually a minor judicial officer, but became a dictator. Result, the United States had its own despots in the time of the great dictators.

The establishment of the FBI was actually the greatest sin of the democratic United States, because it involves an executive organization, which was under the judiciary and still is under. That is the grossest violation of the principle of separation of powers, there is.

There was also resistance in the U.S., there are old press reports that the FBI has been compared to the Gestapo of the Third Reich.

To revamp the poor image, Hoover made a sort of federal police from his agency. The greatest sensation was aroused by the case of the kidnapping of the Lindberg baby. It is still not clear whether the broader offender had something to do, or whether Hoover had staged everything.

There is in American history took a lot more spectacular incidents in connection with the secret services. Even worse, it was with the creation of the CIA.

This secret service emerged from the military intelligence of the Second World War. Before the FBI had taken together with the military intelligence with Italian-born criminals' connection to the Sicilian Mafia. With their help, the invasion of Italy in the Second World War was coordinated.

To ensure that the long war between the FBI and the American Mafia was finished, was the causing havoc at the time of Prohibition. Since that time, criminal organizations are hardly to be distinguished from secret services. Both commit terrible crimes without being prosecuted.

More people around the world with absolute certainty, many times been killed by the secret services, as acts of terrorism. In addition, it guarantees a lot of terrorist attacks on the account of the secret services.

There is therefore no question when the Humane system is ever introduced, secret services must be absolutely forbidden in peacetime.

A preventive counterterrorism is not necessary, because alone in the road to die in a year, more people have died than ever terrorist attacks.

1.8. Data Security

Closely connected with the secret services is data protection. Today's privacy violations are enormous. Citizens' data are collected worldwide. This is all done under the guise of protecting national security, the fight against terrorism or other flimsy pretexts.

In truth, these data are collected for the sale. This results in huge profits. Used are this data from industry to consumer analysis or staff planning positions. Candidates for higher positions will be screened. Also for other areas, these data are used illegally.

However, the most important use is the most completely unknown. This is the use of these data for the calculation of future developments. Nowadays, you can close by the changing of consumption and leisure habits of people in the future. This is primarily used by large financial groups, as this can create securities with best possible returns.

Should it one day succeed, the primacy of politics to restore, this practice should be stopped quickly.

However, the person should be protected mainly. Institutions should be more transparent. Also there should be no protection for machines.

Today, for example, for the evaluation of characteristics of a car also applies strict rules as for the automatic detection of faces which are taken by cameras. The former should be allowed to the State without restriction. The second option should be banned in public places.

1.8.1 Informer

Until the 20th Century were people which collect informations about other people called "Informer".

Then they became informants or „to informal employees" as she called the Secret Service of the former GDR.

Today, there are these spies less; they have been replaced by computer programs. However, one knows their names also. These are, for example, Names, such as Google, Facebook, Twitter, Apple, etc.

Without any real spies but it does not work, these are all working for secret services, of which there are plenty of. Such services are operated not only by states. One of the oldest of them, is guided by the pseudo-religion "Scientology". It is called OSA (Office of Special Affairs). Scientology is known primarily for the two flagships, the actor "John Travolta" and "Tom Cruise".

However, we coming back to the spies. These automated services do not collect any specific data, but will draw anything on what people do. Every phone call, every email, every visit of Internet sites are registered and collected in databases.

Similarly, movement profiles are collected from persons via GPS and mobile phone. Thus one can also detect the leisure behavior of the people directly.

Another option are the many store cards, credit cards, so that the current consumption can also be personalized. Introducing the new IBAN - numbers was mainly enforced for this purpose.

The data are further used mainframes. For example, currently has the most powerful financial company "Black Rock" one of the most powerful computer systems in order to analyze future trends early. BlackRock is a shadow banking and manages four trillion U.S. dollars.

1.9. Immigration

To understand the true motives and reasons for the migration, you should first read the business section. Indeed, it is primarily economic reasons for migration. Nevertheless, it is a political issue.

As in many areas, the crowds are with a variety of false information to be manipulated. On the one hand you talk for years of a lack of skilled workers. Secondly, others claim that immigrants would take away the residents work.

Both claims are largely false.

The Austrian economy has always forms enough skilled workers. If somewhere a shortage of skilled labor would be, then this would be evidenced by the increasing demand, raise wages in this area immediately to the level. Just the opposite has happened. In the last 30 years are as good as all industries dropped to the collective wage level.

The immigrants threaten jobs for nationals only if the policy tolerates illegal low wages. This is in Austria hardly happened in Germany a little more. And it is still happening. On the whole, however, the companies pay the collective wage, so this competition is only a small extent.

The truth, however, you can hardly hear. The real reason why we need immigrants does not exist in their capacity as workers, but in their capacity as a consumer. Without immigration, our economies stagnate.

Immigration is the most important factor for economic growth. The poorer and consumer hungry they are, the better for the forecasts.

Japan has no immigration allowed. That is why this country has the world's highest public debt, as only sovereign debt where they prevent deflation. In other words, the economy shrinks.

For several years, there is more or less consensus in the political camps. We are a country of immigrants, but few know why.

Our current monetary and economic system may be best to delay its collapse with the current conditions.

These realities are politically not for sale, that's why no one talks about it.

The given procedure: The decreasing consumption-saturated population year after year by an increasing population, with higher birth rate, is replaced. This gives us growth, nothing else, apart from short-term up and down once.

The switch to the humane money would end this monstrous necessity, because the new system does not require growth to its survival.

For me, as a reformer, is this monstrosity is not a tragedy, it just amazes me when traditionalists and tradition-conscious parties accept this so.

Likely motive should be here the own career awareness and greed for profit.

1.10. Development aid

Due to the current development aid a small fraction of that amount to get the so-called "developing countries" back, which was previously robbed them of our commodity groups.

There are mainly petroleum, aluminium and copper producers, which have made the practice of everyday life.

These companies commit such crimes to the world of the indigenous population; a list would go beyond the contents of this book, so I ask the readers to inform them about, at least.

Again, the introduction of the Human money would create immediate remedy. Of course, such a thing can only happen with armed support. The corrupt regimes in developing countries are associated with the company in a criminal gang.

2. Economy

Unfortunately include the economics of those disciplines in which intentional misinformation are becoming commonplace.

This discipline shares this fate with several other branches of knowledge. These include climate research, which often encounters powerful counter-interests in the economy. And the health sector, there is mostly about pollutants or drugs which are injurious to health and are obscured by raw materials or pharmaceutical companies. And the historian. Especially on issues of recent history. Unfortunately, the journalism, the time of courageous journalists seems to be coming to an end, what is the biggest catastrophe of all the examples is.

In the economic sector, it concerns mainly the financial sector and the national economy. Often completely reliable knowledge is called into question. There are occasionally so-called experts who present the most hair-raising findings. And unfortunately, there are always innocent followers of such theses. Of course, this also represents a form of corruption

As in all disciplines, one can also appeal to all concerned here only, but please think for yourself in order to be manipulation resistant.

2.1. Distribution of assets

Should the political powers of the earth again someday develop something a little more decorum and seek justice, this can only happen through economic reforms. This may be seen by a brief look at the global distribution of wealth.

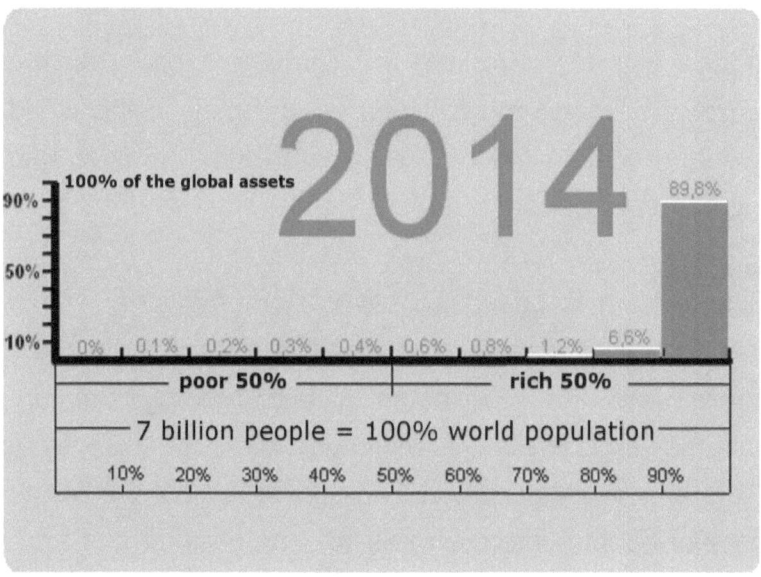

The high proportion of assets in the richest 10% is obtained mainly by the poor countries of the world. There usually possess the richest 10% nearly 100% of all assets. The industrialized countries are usually between 60% and 80%.

Currently, move assets around the world, more and more toward the upper 10%. Only a reversal of this development can provide a just peace on earth.

Without the large financial corporations to crush and install a new monetary system there is no real reform. The EU has still the power to put into their economy in this.

If one were to introduce the Humane money, so the euro in a short time for reserve currency of the world would, because the new system creates the EU rapid economic superiority.

The system is based on several automatisms. These control loops mainly produce stable prices, inflation, there is no more. Furthermore, a staggering minimum income is generated. A minimum wage is linked to it. This all used the central bank. With full control of the money supply, interest rates and purchasing power, a defined basket of products is kept as expensive in the long term.

2.2. Money

Still, most people consider the paper money and coins as the only form of their money. It is generally believed the National Bank prints all the money and gives it to the state and the private banks which then on-lend to companies and individuals. In addition, assume a lot of people that their savings are awarded as loans.

Of all them tune as much as anything.

Paper money and coins make up just 3% of our money. 97%, almost everything is pure bank money and exists only in the computers and balance sheets of the banks.

Money to lend comes neither from the deposits of savers still of the National Bank. There shall be created with the booking of a loan. The bank only has a duty to report to the central bank and has to prove 1% of the loan amount as minimum security.

The total money supply of the earth is to the amount payable on a loan more. With the repayment of the loan, the money supply decreases again. In practice, however, the money supply is increasing, that is, the amount of money for new loans is always greater than the amount of money paid back for loans.

Since loans always require real securities, the money supply is primarily propagated by new-financial assets, ie, assets in the economy is growing faster than worthless old assets.

A growth of the economy is with this current system, therefore, necessary in the long term. Does not grow the economy, the result is immediate deflation.

Japan practiced this already more than 20 years by using its sovereign debt is constantly increasing. With these debts this state produces a minimal growth, which corresponds to the amount of interest. Thus Japan has by far the highest public debt of all economies.

100% of the money, bring the savers to the bank is created by the banks in the financial market. That is, the bank buys securities for; this is called also proprietary trading by banks, as opposed to trading for bank customers.

Securities are stocks, bonds, certificates, warrants and other derivatives. In the securities divisions of the big banks now derivatives are created with such a variety, a real clear view has here no more. Not even the authorities, which should monitor all of this. Such papers are recognized as assets. Thus, banks have the ability to create almost any number of collateral for new loans.

Stocks, bonds, and insurance policies, contracts and many other papers and contracts serve the derivatives departments in the big banks as raw materials from which they produce their virtual values. Quite deliberately, this industry uses the word "industry" and "products" to give their creations a semblance of value created.

This inflation of the money supply through virtual assets is anything but healthy for the existence of national economies. Created The acceptance of these papers as security for loans, and creates a huge financial industry. This cancerous growth exists alongside our real economy and lives of their income. Both employers and employees pay each month for this moloch, which is now a huge casino.

Shares, ie shares in the company, along with other papers, such as those as in commodity trading, that the only securities that represent a true real value. The restriction to such papers as credit protection would be a good first step towards reform.

In the long term, however, only a reform of the creation of money in today's society, which has quite worthy of protection pages, saves them from ruin. That is, the creation of money by private banks must be stopped. This is due in the future also the nationalization of all central banks, because there are countries whose national banks, completely or partly, in private hands. One of these countries is the United States.

2.3. GDP

The real gross domestic product of an economy reflects the economic performance of a year. It arises when one frees nominal GDP by the price increase, which is, divided by the rate of inflation.
GDP$_{(real)}$=GDP$_{(nominal)}$ / Price Index

GDP includes only goods destined for final consumption. Other products and services that are produced and delivered to the economy are not included. These are roughly about half of all freight a year.

By dividing the GDP by the population, we obtain a comparison value that indicates how efficiently an economy works. The higher the GDP / capita the more goods creates the economy at the same power. Or vice versa, the economy can create the same amount of goods with different high cost. Therefore there is also the productivity again.

Some examples for better understanding.

Example 1: Increases an economy wages, for example, through wage negotiations by social partners. Then, the economy can only respond with an increase in prices or a productivity improvement. If there is no increase in productivity, there remains real GDP, despite higher money supply, as high as the previous year. The total wage increase was then converted into inflation. Unless demand is rising strongly. Unfortunately, this hardly happened lately, because the majority of the population has no need. Only immigration can our current system to ensure economic growth.

Example 2: Decreases the legislature to taxation, the economy can reduce prices. Productivity and sales will hardly change, because only rich citizens benefit. The money supply decreases. Real GDP remains the same again. The tax cut was implemented into deflation. However, exports also be stimulated, which increases the sales of products. Depending on whether this also creates more work, or not, will also increase by more wage payments, the purchasing power, or not.

Example 3: The Legislature shall establish a minimum wage. The economy reacts again with price increases. However, the minimum wage increases the purchasing power immediately, which in turn increases the demand. More production also usually increases productivity, so that prices fall again. GDP remains the same again, but it was redistributed from the rich to the employees.

All three examples show the importance of purchasing power in an economy. The resource-rich countries in Africa could easily increase their GDP if they would increase the purchasing power of the poor. This would allow for the right development aid.

The Humane money would ensure, through its systematic automatisms for adequate world gross domestic product.

2.4. Interest

Interest rates have always been the most controversial topic of economics. The Prophet Muhammad has forbidden interest, because even then the poorer population was exploited it.

There were and are always systems that do away with the problem of interest, there has never been but lasting success. The current system in Islamic banks is a mixture of a little more decency and religious alibi. Strictly speaking, these are just too clever renaming of customary practices. For example, a loan for a home purchase is by the bank with subsequent rental. The same is also available in ordinary banks, the so-called lease-purchase financing.

However, there are also numerous worlds territorial systems which operate without interest, mostly these are swap meets, which, however, never really prevail. They usually remain limited regionally or only for short times of emergency operation.

In order to understand our present system, best viewed the entire money supply on Earth. There are for this sum of both creditors and debtors. Both have the same amount that a debt, the other IOUs. These bonds are nothing more than our money.

However, money does not stand alone; it represents assets which are present on the planet. There should not be more money than there are assets. However, is precisely the problem in today's money system? Due to the unbridled creation of structured securities created fictitious assets, which are then used again as collateral with new money creation. This means that our entire global money supply inflates from year to year continues on.

The 0% financing: Hardly anyone believes that a bank could live if she gets any interest on their credit awarded. To the surprise of many, but it is possible. The seller suggests anything on the sales price to allow this form of financing. How can something like this work?

This is a complex process by which the bank does not get the interest from the borrower, but by the financial market. As a credit fee, however, hide whatever interest, but these are not higher than the usual discount or the credit card fee.

So how exactly does this process?

Such institutions always emit structured documents, which multiply with leverage these low interest rates. This, of course, the risk is multiplied. These risks carry the purchasers of such securities.

Derivatives departments of large banks use loans as underlying assets. They are like raw materials from which they produce their structured securities for them. You also do this with stocks, bonds, insurance policies, certificates, contracts, options and other derivatives. From pledged values, new values are created again and again, now these fictitious values exceed by far all real values, which makes it always comes back to crises. Namely, if waning confidence in such papers, the price drops, so that the investors panic sell such securities, making the value falls further. With the artistic value but also always falls the underlying, so about real estate loans are no longer covered. Usually it comes then to the auction of objects. Usually, however, creates an unnecessary bankruptcy of a company.

The issuer of such securities sold expectations, nothing else. By complex risk assessments variety of future developments are interrelated and offered as a safe asset in the market. Investors buy as long as the expectations are met. It involves huge pyramid schemes, or in simpler terms, to combined betting systems. There are always losers in these bets, but these are not the issuers of the securities.

Interest are the lure for these securities, the higher they are, the more coveted the products. But who ultimately pays this interest?

This will be paid by all those that create value. These are both entrepreneurs and workers. Your entire value created is exactly by the amount worth less to get the investors collectively the interest on their papers. Or conversely said. Their products would be exactly by the amount worth more to skim off the investors. This is a tremendous cash flow, which is a redistribution of the diligent to investors.

Looked at another way, the global financial market creates a formidable inflation, which is intercepted by the real economy through constant increase in productivity. Without this operation, we would have a huge deflation in the world's low wages.

Popular economists such as Dirk Müller, Harald Leisch and others criticize the system of private money creation for years. However, it is often grossly exaggerated. It will serve as the sole justification always progressive function of compounding system. In truth, there are many factors in addition to the interest that make today's debt money system the main cause of strife in the world.

The dispute over the culmination

This contention among a small minority of economists now takes as 100 years. He goes back to Silvio Gesell, a brilliant thinkers of the last century.

It is about the compound interest culminating with the passage of time. However, the bad thing about this dispute is not the case itself, but the small minority of economists.

This even has a name. His name is TINA (There Is No Alternative). This name says that economists simply do not deal with an alternative to the current system. Take it to university professors, without ever having heard the name of Silvio Gesell.

Therefore, is a prerequisite for a solution, the consciousness of the problem. Subsequently, each state must the most important tool of democracy, the money put back under state control. This is what makes the Humane monetary system.

The Humane money does not create the interest from, but it ends the private creation of money, which banks, which at the same grant loans and issue securities can not create any more money themselves.

Also, is billed monthly in the human system and destroyed if necessary money or scooped. These are based on **human value**, the **number of inhabitants** and the **base period**. Lending has here a secondary influence.

2.5. Save money

The Tale of the happy savers will give people told 400 years and the vast majority of people still believe it.

Each time has its own methods to deceive the public.

This machination of high finance was good until today supported by the policy. In truth, it is pure poison for society when money is by saving a commodity. Because money has a completely different purpose

Money should always flow and stay only for short periods of time in one place. Therefore, it would be best in the final analysis, if the policy would prohibit by law the temporal binding of saving money.

The motive for this continuous lie is relatively simple. In earlier times, it was the most profitable way to get to cheap money. This was then invested profitably. This reason has not changed to this day, only the financial sector has now much more alternatives.

A reform of the banking system should be cleanly separated in the current sector and in the credit sector. These areas should be well of personnel and accounting law entirely separate. The FMA (Financial Market Supervision) would have to monitor this strictly.

In the human system, only the cash credit sector gets money from the National Bank. This money is used exclusively for lending, so this sector thrives on the fees, commissions and interest rate differentials. This is also in today's credit being largely the case.

By contrast, the current sector thrives on the money buffer of current accounts. The collective management of many current accounts gives rise to a certain amount of money, which remains permanently intact and is invested by the Institute for profit. The longer account transactions are carried out with a time delay, the higher this amount of money, the higher of the income for the bank.

One can only advise any user of current accounts to select the most bank, because most banks and book their clients high fees by direct debit. Although, they earning through the short-term investment. No do not be dissuaded, even if you pay at the same bank loans. One has nothing to do with the other. The Austrian Chamber of Labour offers a bank's computer to find the best account.

As an alternative to saving money the girobanks offer other forms of saving. Both in the future as well as today, everyone should be clear about the motivation of the Bank. Each girobank has an inherent self-interest in saving money in order to speculate on the market itself. Any advice by the Bank should therefore be consumed with due suspicion.

For the future, it would be most important, if the company shares, such shares would be distributed to the width of mass. This would be the most ideal form of saving. These, however, would first company law be reformed, because today draw supervisory boards and boards of a large portion of the company profits from. This is actually, today, a scam of shareholders. In addition, the stock prices move nowadays very often far away from the actual value, which is on the supremacy of individual players in the major financial casino.

That is why the human system also requires a new legal form for business. This form of business is called SSC.

2.6. Taxation
Today's global tax systems are mainly a. Unjust and complicated. It is not at all surprising if large envy prevails on the strata of the population of the rich.

In many parts of the world the wealthy not find real happiness more, because they have to be constantly worried about their safety. You can no longer move freely and enjoy the benefits of their assets.

They would have to make in the hand for fairer tax systems and so to regain peace.

In the Human System two taxes are absolutely necessary, a third is attached to political control.

Before a word for wealth tax. It arises only envy and encourages this as well. They should not be allowed in the humane system. Assets should be no shame, but the result of motivation. However, this requires a control system that is shrinking fast in performance deficiency inherited wealth.

2.6.1 Inheritance Tax

That is why the estate tax is the most important control in the new monetary system. It varies by an automatism. Bad economy end regions automatically have a high inheritance tax.

Corruption will always exist as long as there are people. The inheritance tax is in humane system is an automatic corrective, by corrupt upper classes heavily taxed when generational change. Decent economy end regions can inherit a large part of their assets to their children.

The inheritance tax is described in more detail in the section "Human money."

2.6.2. Income Tax

The second tax is the **income tax**. This tax is not calculated any more by the holdings but by computer programs in the Ministry of Finance.

Unemployed income can also be captured, such as income from labour.

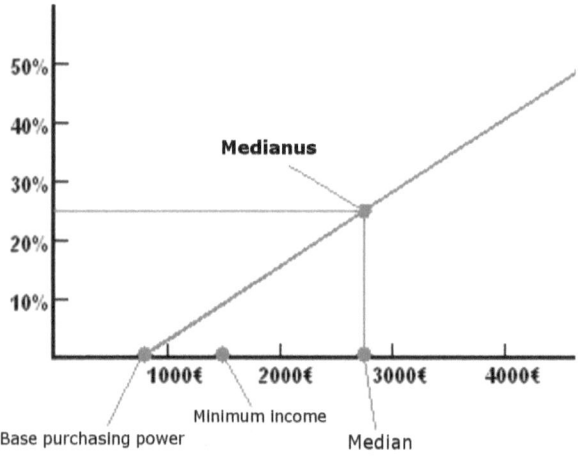

Medianus

Any income over the basic purchasing power is taxed. From a tax rate of 0%, a line is drawn. This line runs by the Medianus to them 49% height achievedly .Then the line makes a crease.

The bend is caused by a mathematical factor.

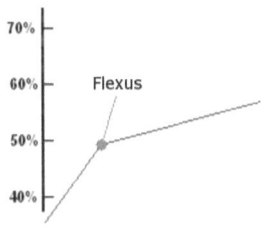

This factor is part of a formula whose result must satisfy two conditions.

1. Higher incomes pay more taxes than lower ones.

2. The net amount of higher incomes is always higher than that of smaller incomes.

Both the **Medianus**, and the **Flexus** are the values which are determined by the policy. It concerns budgetary adjustment screws that are changed on a proposal from the Minister of Finance of the legislature.

Any income of a person is detected, regardless of where the income comes from. Whether the payment is established by the sale of property, through wage for labor, by income from securities, by speculation, by interest income, rental income or through other, is not a concern.

Compensatory allowance

Marginal labour income not only get the full basis of purchasing power, but also required by a mathematical formula, a compensatory payment is calculated. Incomes from labour power below the minimum wage will always receive a compensation payment, but less and less, the closer they get to the minimum wage, they never achieve with it completely.

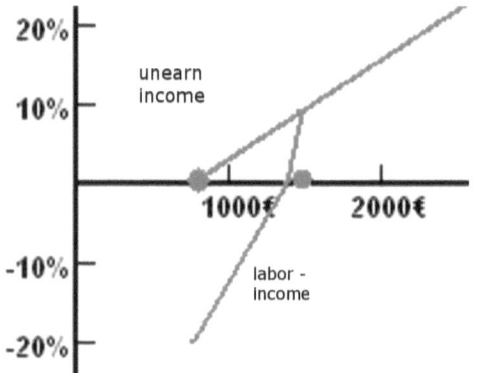

This seems a little complicated at first glance, on closer examination, however, outweigh the benefits.

In the old system unearned incomes were subsidized, this is reversed in the humane system. Labour income are subsidized and thus discriminated against unearned income.

For example, young families with two children, the basis of purchasing power 4 times. Parents can work with several hours still raise this income. Stay below the minimum wage, they receive the allowance.

This also has implications for reducing undeclared work. For example, an assistant in the restaurant business is their wages reported to the tax office in the new system, since it is increased by this regulation.

As you can later read under the section "VAT", such works are also exempt from VAT, so there is no more reason to work illegally.

The compensation only affects younger people without inherited wealth, because older already have an unearned income.

Of course, applies the minimum wage for part-time work. This hourly rate is calculated by dividing the minimum monthly wage by monthly hours of standard working hours.

In addition, there are no exceptions, neither for donations, church contributions or other things. If the state wants to subsidize something like that. Not by settling of the taxes, but by legal direct payments Any subsidy should be transparent and understandable. This transparency means public access for all citizens.

The tax calculation is no longer in the factories. Gross wages are paid cash on current accounts. For each bank account, there is a reporting obligation of the inputs to the tax office. There, the income tax is calculated automatically.

Every citizen has so a revenue account with the financial, which summarizes all the inputs of the current accounts of a person. The Tax Office also receives an automatic debit authorization to deduct the tax. Also, the tax equalization is performed automatically by the tax office.

Banking secrecy over the Monetative is completely abolished. Data flows from the Monetative are strictly controlled.

Tax equalization

A tax period is 5 years, the income tax is balanced over this period. However, the age of 5 can also shorten. Does anyone have a whole month no taxable income, such as illness, vacation, or other reasons as the tax equalization is performed on the last day of the previous month. The new period shall not begin until the month of recovery.

Report To control the banks, the companies wage payments to the tax office.

Companies need payment for employees settle separately; this may not be deducted from the salary. This concerns, for example, private uses of company vehicles, canteen meals and the like.

However, this is also true in the opposite case. Kind of employees shall be compensated by the company.

This is especially true for the ride of employees to and from work site. These costs are to be borne by the company. The official mileage or the cost of the public transport network are to be paid in full to the employee. This is also not a salary component and must also be paid separately. This means that even state commuter allowance and the like no longer necessary.

Private cash receipts are also notifiable, or be paid into their own checking account.

Of course, it also comes in the humane system to evasion, this can never prevent. The system can do that, just as today, to cope if there is a proper prosecution.

Both taxes, inheritance and income tax, serve the social balance, so additional social security contributions are in the human system is no longer necessary, these two taxes are the social system on the input side.

2.6.3. VAT

The third tax is the **sales tax** or **VAT**. She has no social component and should serve for the control. Therefore, there should be no fixed tax rates for this tax type, but product-specific tax rates. Thus, the policy has much more influence on the prices of various products and can thus promote or inhibit their use.

Here the imagination of policy is required. For example, one product, which partially caused by slave labor, or those which are partly caused by environmental degradation, taxing higher than those that were produced socially and environmentally sustainable.

On services, there should be no VAT, this will only lead to increased undeclared work and more expensive the work of small and medium-sized enterprises unnecessary. This could free the entire gastronomy of tax payments then, for example. For each consumer would then open the gastronomy of the end user, a deduction of pretax would also be eliminated.

As long as it, in addition to the SSC, is corporations, including corporate and trade taxes are necessary.

Thus, this simple control system is operating efficiently, cashless payment transactions will be further expanded. Companies are allowed to operate among themselves without cash only. Cash is only for private consumption, so that people can enjoy their leisure time in an uncontrolled manner.

2.7. SSC
The **S**ocial **S**hare **C**ompany

The Human Money needs a new form of company, so that the general population can save real values. In addition, the **SSC**(**S**ocial **S**hare **C**ompany) provides long term, the primacy of politics restored.

The SSC is the stock company similar, but with some serious differences.

1. Have voting rights only to natural persons, Institutional Shares have no vote in the election of the Supervisory Board.

2. People have from a holding of shares worth 600% median active and passive voice.

3. Each voter has only one vote regardless of the number of units. The right to vote is not transferable.

4. From passive suffrage persons be excluded with incompatibilities to the company interest.

5. The election of the Supervisory Board are held annually.

6. At least 20% of SSC Shares must be in privately owned by individuals, because only they have in this type of society the right to vote. Although shares in institutional ownership receive the full dividend, but have no voting rights.

7. Shares are sold or bought only through a State Exchange. Only through inheritance takes place a change of ownership without Exchange.

8. At the SSC stock market there are buying priorities. With the same buy limit an individual will be ranked against a legal person. Furthermore, has a buyer with previously owned more shares, against a buyer with less pre-owned shares in the cold. Furthermore, buyers are ranked residing in the economy before others.

9. The Board has no authority over the company's shares, they may also not be a component payroll of employees.

10. SSC does not pay corporate taxes nor trade taxes. Also, the company's profit is not taxed. This will make them attractive to companies. The tax is only the employee's wages and the shareholders over dividends, both subject to income tax.

11. There are no salaries or compensation for Supervisory Board members. Only expenses are paid by the company.

12. Only the Supervisory Board is responsible for salaries of the board members or capital by new issue of shares.

In practice, boards that distribute high dividends, also elected to the Supervisory Board. Or vice versa, others who earn little dividend will be removed quickly.

Individual companies, associations and cooperatives are automatically converted to a SSC above a certain level of revenue. However, on the stock exchange they have to only if the shares are traded. This may also be new issues to increase capital.

The SSC Exchange also supports **start-ups**, by selling shares before the foundation and supports the foundation. The founder requires a minimum capital of 600%

median. Finding a business idea enough buyers to cover the budgeted capital requirement, there is no foundation and the stock market refunded back the investment.

Financially, no money flows without state control, each cash flow across national borders via the central bank. The currency conversion is done while fully automatic and runs without time delay, free in the background.

2.7.1. Election of the Supervisory Board

The purpose of the Supervisory Board is the control of the company, as well as the cases of policy decisions such as the appointment of board members, the salaries of management, major investment projects, capital increases, etc.

2.7.2. Election process

This election process describes the choice of the supervisory board of a SSC. However, it can also be used for any political choice.

1. A few days before the election, every voter can identify with the election program. He can change his phone number, the constituency and

the PIN. These data are strictly protected from tampering.

2. During the election, only the server of the constituencies access to the electoral program. This prevents overloading of the main server.

3. The election is held on a certain day, in a specified period of time.

4. With the start of the election of the Returning Officer enters a password to access the database choice. After only has the election program to access the data. Previously reviewed by a trained notary the correctness of the database.

5. The election program sends the data to the voters to the server of the constituencies.

6. The choice can be done from any computer with Internet access. The voters logs on with his PIN to the server of his constituency.

7. Even public offices provide ready devices. On request there to attend a sworn election officials of the election. Also a mobile poll workers is conceivable.

8. The server checks the authorization of the constituency. The voter will be forwarded to the electoral program.

9. After selecting the candidates the voter requests a transaction number (TAN). It chooses between SMS and voice announcements.

10. The election program sends an SMS or a voice announcement to the phone number. In it the elected candidate and the TAN are included. This TAN is valid for 2 minutes.

11. The voter verifies the correctness and returns the TAN. This he confirms his choice. The manifesto also confirms the correct choice.

12. In Inaccuracies voter selects between multiple causes and confirmed without entering the TAN. He reports the error even in his constituency and leads the election again by.

13. The electoral program saves the TAN and the persons elected. All compounds of TAN and voters are deleted at the end of the election. Until then, each voter may modify its election by a new one.

14. The server of constituencies allows only a limited number of times.

15. In the election protocol, only the TAN and the selected candidates.

16. At the end of the election, the election program calculates the election results and published it.

This modern election process has several distinct advantages over conventional elections.

1. It is far cheaper.

2. No delay by counting of ballots.

3. The voter experiences with the confirmation whether he has chosen valid, so there is no accidental Invalid voters more.

4. Provable monitoring of the election by the voters via the confirmation. The TAN system identifies the voters clearly when a fraud.

5. No human errors.

6. The voter can participate from anywhere on Earth.

Should this process be used for a political choice, as stores of the voting machines, in addition to the TAN, also the constituency, the municipality or the county, depending on how exactly you want to capture the distribution of voters.

2.7.3. Meeting of the supervisory board

An official of the Ministry of Economic Affairs attends every meeting. For smaller businesses these sessions will be held at the site of the Chamber of Commerce.

Again, there are laws that prevent that decisions are made to the detriment of the company or the shareholders.

The officer is subject to confidentiality, he intervenes only in case of possible malfeasance. He prevents such an early stage. He responds to questions on the advice of the Supervisory Board. He has no right to vote on decisions.

The main tasks of the Supervisory Board are made in the order of the board members and the capital of the company.

In order to finance larger investments new shares are issued. The sale of these shares, the new investments is financed. Loans are used only for bridges and for small investments.

There are no salaries or compensation for Supervisory Board members. Only expenses are paid by the company.

2.7.4 SSC with the public interest

For companies with public interests a special form of SAG is created. These are companies which are mostly funded by donations, grants or membership fees.

These are associations, political parties, charities, hospitals, etc.

For these institutions, a minimum price for a share which, for example € 5 - can be. Increases the price rises above the minimum price, the Institute is a normal SSC. Until the price falls back on the minimum price.

Generate, for example, Clubs a profit, they are temporarily ordinary companies.

Only this special form may limit the potential buyers of shares. A list of members is at the SSC Exchange.

2.7.5. SSC - Exchange

The SSC market is a public market under the guidance of the Ministry of Economy. It is less volatile than other exchanges.

Speculation with SSC values will be less lucrative than those with equity values. Trading is just like any other stock exchanges Trader, usually this will be the Bank, in which you have your checking account.

SSC values of a country can only be traded on a stock exchange this. However, exchange trader you in every place in the world, buy and send sales orders.

SSC shares can be bought and sold on the stock exchange. The only exception is inheritances. Inheritance process also performs the change of ownership of SSC shares.

Each transaction sets the price (value of a share) on the purchase price of this transaction commits.

A limit is mandatory. For purchase orders, this is the price ceiling at which the transaction is to be carried out.

For sales orders, this is the bottom price at which the transaction is to be carried out.

To overlap two limits of sales and purchase order, as it comes to the transaction. The new price is always the one that comes closest to the old.

Buy and sell orders are sorted and processed in a list according to priorities.

<u>The priorities are</u>:
No consideration to institutional buy orders, unless 20% of the units are privately owned.

Buyers whose main residence is in the region of the company, before buyers outside the region.

Natural person, to institutional buyers.

Buyers with less shares previously owned, with prior buyers previously owned more shares.

2.7.6. Effects

Individual and family are converted at the latest with the death of the principal owner in a SSC. Due to the tax advantages but this is almost always used to be. The units may continue to remain in the family, when all the heirs are in agreement, then the company is not public.

Most go for generational change but by the inheritance shares to the State lost. This sold those shares as soon as possible. This fall the most family on the stock market. In most cases, however, the main legacy is subsequently appointed to the Board of the company.

The dividends of SSC values are much higher than those of equities, because corrupt supervisory boards and dizzying directors' salaries, there are not there. The company's profits are to make full dividends for the company owners. The dividend will be the same for each share, including shares that are located in institutional ownership.

2.8. Insurance

The entire insurance industry is completely fused with the investment sector of the financial industry today. Securing of price fluctuations by buying or selling derivatives, it is called in the jargon "hedging" is basically just an insurance.

An insurance contract is nothing more than a Protection against future risks. Although he is not as complex, such as futures, options or swaps, but basically it serves a similar purpose.

This industry thrives on complex bets on the future, she is so worldwide by more money than all other sectors combined.

First, our modern economic system requires certain mechanisms to hedge risks, on the other hand it is nowadays exploited downright of this industry, the benefits are out of proportion to the damage that inflicts this industry.

With the introduction of the Human money, there must also come to far-reaching reforms that range.

This is done by converting all the insurance, banking, gaming companies, investment companies and similar enterprises in a SSC.

The legislature decides to a separate law, which regulates this conversion affected are all defined company based within the country.

Branches of corporations are not exempt. These are legally separate from the parent company. Although the SSC shares retained by the parent company, but it has no voting rights in the formation of the Supervisory Board. Therefore, at least 20% of the shares in the SSC Exchange.

After the sale of the shares, a new Board is elected. This will then appoint a new board or confirms the existing board of directors.

2.9. Temporary work

The hiring out of labor was an everyday practice in the European economy. Especially in Germany, this development led to a two-class society, among the employed persons. Austria protects temporary workers a little better, but even here we can speak of a similar development.

The industry of temporary employment is today a large proportion of total employment. Many companies meet with agency staff not only need tips off, but constantly keep a personal stock of temporary workers. In many cases admissions staff will be carried out only with prior lending.

Where the temporary work agency would be most useful, namely in the public sector, agency staff are hard to find. It would make sense because just there, mostly due to lack of competition, there is often an incredible lack of power. Austria could save only by the substitute of 80% of the contract employee by lending manpower many million euro yearly in administrative costs.

One can discuss whether temporary work on this scale is generally necessary for reasons of justice, there is no reason to exclude the public sector it.

In Austria, the sector of public employees was up in the 70s, a low-wage sector. For these jobs were irredeemable. Whether it was a cop, train staff, teachers, postal official or magistrate clerk, you had to settle for about 60% of the wage of a skilled worker in the private sector content.

The real wages of the private sector have shrunk since that time. How to earn today's skilled workers usually about the same, often even less than a comparable worker in the public sector. And although the protection in the state administration remained the same.

2.10. Pension system

Because of the incredibly stupid actions of policy in this area, I think it is appropriate, first to make a few basics of economics. These foundations have now probably lost a lot of economists from the eyes.

<u>Basics:</u>

Every economy produces annually products and services for consumption by the population.

This assembly is referred to as GDP (gross domestic product), which depicts this overall cake mathematically.

Through the annual net income each person receives a personal share of this pie.

Whatever the expert of the various institutes gives this or that the prognosis for future economic development, if he and his computer program does not consider these three sentences, his statements have no useful value.

As is already evident from the definition of consumption is the essential element of this. Although, the work does not play an important role, however, as other means of production. Whether this GDP is produced with 70% participation of the population or with only 20% participation is completely irrelevant. The important thing is that enough people are available for the necessary work.

Money saved goes directly to the financial industry, it reaches the real economy no longer, because it remains in the circulation of the investment industry, which thus further blows up year after year. While it flows into the GDP, because this sector produces yes. However, only fictitious values for investors. The real economy is growing so that in any way.

Abroad consumed the money in the economy is not harmful as long as long as enough foreigners consume us, because that the trade balance is compensated.

Who is even close to being able to think of something economically, which should now also the absurdity of the talk about the pension system is clear. Economically, it is completely irrelevant whether a 63 year old works or a 20 year old. It is only important that all jobs are done.

Politically, however, it is not irrelevant, because the young people need a meaningful future.

Also irrelevant is whether a pensioner receives his income from the control pot, or from a PAYG system is. It is only important that he gets enough so that the purchasing power does not drop.

For employees, it is completely irrelevant whether a part of her prints taxes or insurance premiums are called. It makes a difference neither for him nor for the total economy.

Therefore, after the introduction of the Human money you need no pension system. However, it requires the SSC already described, so that busy people can save up a higher income. The system is suffering in any way, though many people live only from the minimum security. The formation of a labor shortage, so immediately decreases the amount of the basic purchasing power, which again more people in employment.

It is the task of politics to divide the necessary work meaningful. The Humane monetary system requires, unlike today, no unconditional economic growth. However, each region will also endeavor not to fall over the other. Even then receive residents from regions with higher economic power higher incomes.

For those readers who still do not understand these simple facts, a very simple idea to understand.

Imagine, only theoretically, all the work could be done machines. The entire economy could produce all of our goods without a handle a human being.

Even then we would all goods for consumption are available. Without a job, of course you need another distribution system for the produced goods.

This example has nothing to do with reality, it is only the simplicity of the economy make it clear to.

2.11. Unemployment

Generally nowadays refers to those persons registered as unemployed, the unemployment benefits or social assistance.

This definition can not and I will not connect. For me, these are all people who make no contribution to the emergence of annual GDP.

There is of course no black-and-white division. Almost all people have at least a small part in the creation of annual GDP. A minimum pensioner will be treated according to my definition, a social welfare in general.

I am concerned, however, more to the unemployed people with assets. This group of people is indeed much smaller than those without wealth, although they receive from the annual national income a much higher proportion than the poor unemployed. There are also, of course, no precise figures, but the factor is somewhere between 100:1 and 1000:1. That is, if the poor unemployed get 1 million euro, flows to the wealthy unemployed 1 billion euros.

The only difference is in the method of payment. Some are funded by the tax pot, the other on the financial market. Pure economically this makes no difference; the public perception is, however, always focused on the lower portion of the money poor unemployed.

We first clarify the question of whether unemployment benefits come from the tax pot. All are social, economic seen to equate the social staggered wage and income tax. It is just another label.

You could always save those institutions that manage these funds and pay it. All this could also do the ministries. It would save a lot of administrative costs.

Now we come to the wealthy unemployed. As they come to their part of the big cake? This is also much easier to understand at a macro-economic approach. They get their money through interest on its assets, usually securities. The whole financial industry is struggling, this group of people the best investments for sale. The more successful they are, the lower the wages of workers and the profits of the employer. Economically, it does not matter whether you pay more taxes or receive less pay for his work, the result is the same.

Anyone who is really willing to think through these processes will end up losing not a single word of alleged social parasites from the poor class, because they hurt the economy, in contrast to their rich counterparts, in any way. On the contrary, the higher the amount of their unemployment income is, the more direct purchasing power is produced, which makes the economy grow.

With this mechanism, resource-rich countries in Africa could be quite simple and easy an economic Turbo fire that would give you an incredible boost growth.

2.12. Investment

From € 3.000, - to € 5.000.-on the credit side of the current account, it is appropriate to seek a more profitable form for the surplus.

The savings account no longer makes sense, because even temporally bound saving money usually not achieved in the current interest rate, the inflation rate.

Those who do not want to take care of the invested money, the best buys fund shares or fixed-interest bonds with his bank.

For bonds it is the State or company money as a loan. If the company is insolvent, it can lead to a total loss. So only buy bonds where such a thing can never happen. However, throw quite safe bonds to little return from.

For funds fund managers ensure the highest possible return. However, there are risks by financial crises or bad management. In addition, the fund companies collect veritable administrative fees. However, a total loss is not possible, because even in case of insolvency of the Company, the Shares flow to the rear savers back, but usually at a worse course, and it may lead to losses.

Better than Fund shares, you will thus co-owner of the company. You look for companies which distribute the highest possible dividends. At the same time, however, the performance should not be disregarded.

The only derivative I can recommend put warrants here. In order to compensate for falling prices of a stock. If the price of the shares purchased, the value of the warrant increases. However, one has to also observe the development of the derivative and must not lose sight of the end of the term. You have to study something before definitely get to know this business better.

If you're getting into it, you should exert such an option even once. You buy even with the warrant exercise of the right. Thus one can sell his shares at the agreed price, even if they are currently fallen sharply in price.

In Germany and Austria, some data sheets are to be signed before they can ever execute such transactions. This confirms you several times that you have read the risk warnings. And also understood.

This procedure illustrates very clearly how ridiculous are the claims of some local politicians protection. This often claims to have gambled in ignorance of the risks of public funds.

Once it has been approved for high-risk transactions, it is tempting to make lucrative investments. Especially certificates promise high earnings outlook.

For certificates, one should note that there will be a total loss if the issuer becomes insolvent. The underlying assets of such derivatives are always bearer bonds, that is, the company is leaving his money. What makes them so accurately is often very unclear, particularly in structured securities?

Certificates with reference to an index or "basket" are still reasonable degree of transparency. It is also available with an open runtime, so-called "long-distance runner". Losses are never ruled out with certificates.

If the Human monetary system introduced in the distant future, so then available for investment, the corporate form SSC. Thus, there is a lot more different companies to buy shares. One can then really, without much risk, in the long run save profitable if you acquire the broadest possible range of interests.

Money is no longer saved. Someone who needs the money to consume or invest sold SSC shares, anyone who has money to save, buy SSC shares. Money itself is in the circulation of the real economy.

3. Human Money

Human Money describes a money system which neither allows retail central banks nor retail money creation. The system presents a reform of the monetary system at the turn of the millennium.

The Human monetary system enabled to open the upvaluation and devaluation of different national economies, even when using the same currency. This is made possible due to the so called '**human value**'. In this system, it is not the prices that are fluctuating but the human value.

The work of the central bank thus exists in the main therein the price fluctuations shifting on the human value.

The **human value** is calculated: **gross domestic product (GDP)/per person*base period**

The quantity of money is recooned to a necessary level by the '**base period**'.

The total **quantity of money** of each national economy is calculated: **human value * population figure.**

Monthly balances any central bank, the existing quantity of money from that of the previous month. Depending on the change of the economic power (GDP) or the number of inhabitants, money is thereby destroyed or created.

Each central bank has a defined quantity of money as a safety buffer. Other safeties, such as gold, foreign exchange, etc., do not exist in the human system.

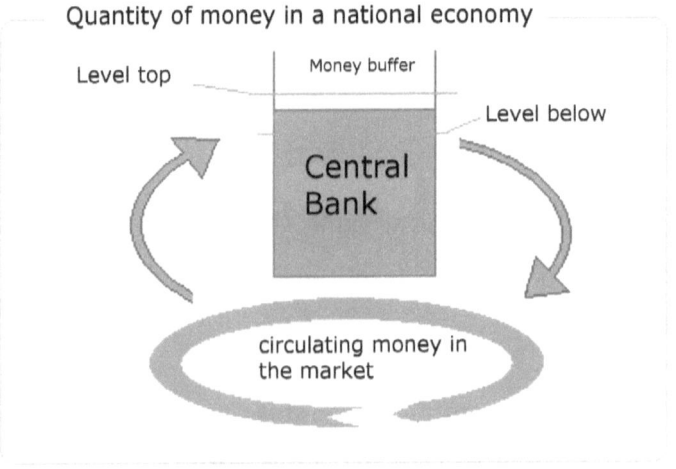

Falls the amount of money supply of the buffer falls below a certain level, the **base period** is increased, so that the level of resources is reached again. Exceeds the monetary amount of the buffer the level cap, the **base period** is shortened. Therefore, new money is defeat or old money is created.

In The Human monetary system works several automatism. One of these with the linking of the **base period** to the **inheritance tax**. The longer the base period, the higher the inheritance tax.

Another automatism regulated the prices. In the Human monetary system, a **defined shopping basket** is kept equally expensive always the medium term. With help of the prime rate, the state interest rate and the basic purchasing power, inflation or deflation no longer exists.

The so called '**basic purchasing power**' represents a guaranteed minimum protection. The height is not determined by social aspects but instead by macroeconomic necessities. This way, the purchasing power of the weaker classes of society is changed. She sways depending on the development of the **median**, humane value and prices.

A **minimum wage** also represents a mandatory component of the Human monetary system. It is calculated: **basic purchasing power * 1.8**

The minimum wage is also divided by the monthly norm working time. This ensures that a **minimum wage per hour** is no longer undermined.

All in all, these key points of the system are defined with that. The Human Money also requires accompanying reforms of the social, economic and tax systems.

3.1. Median

The median is a statistical quantity. In contrast to the average, the median points exactly to the value in the middle, when all values in ascending order stringing together. Thus, the median often deviates greatly from the average. If it is further spoken of the median, it refers to the median income of citizens of a region.

Salaries for politicians and officials, fees, pensions and social benefits should always be specified as a percentage of median. For example, the salary for a politician is 150% median, or e.g. the minimum is 25% median. Changes are no longer necessary, because the median varies anyway; so that justice once found is constantly receive.

3.2. Base period

The base period results from the money supply and the economy of a region at the time of conversion to the human monetary system.

For Germany, this would be the year 2012, an amount of money of about 19, 21 million euros / head divided by GDP / capita of 33,000 euros. This gives a period of 582 years.

Each region will change the base period later, it can vary greatly from region to region.

The base period is directly coupled to inheritance tax. The higher the base period, the higher the inheritance tax. In regions that operate extremely poor, immobile assets be redeployed quickly. There, the upper class can not hold in her own family fortune. In good economic border regions, the assets can be inherited to the next generations.

A region is forced to increase the base period, if the total amount of money would be scarce. To keep the inheritance tax low, every region strives to keep the money supply as short as possible.

3.3. Human value

The human monetary system used to man himself as a base. This basis is called the human value and size is the life's work over several generations.

Calculates this value from the Human gross domestic product, the base period and the number of inhabitants. GDP is divided by the inhabitants of the region and multiplying by the base period. The GDP per capita in 2012 in Germany at about € 33,000. -. This would result in a base period of 582 years, a human value of just over 19 million euros.

It can result in slightly different figures, also, this is not essential. Important are the same conditions for all.

Increases the economic output as increase human value. If the economic power also decreases as the human value. The same happens when you change the number of inhabitants. The central bank makes this adjustment is performed monthly. There is no discretion here, because this value is calculated by clear facts.

3.4. Money supply

The current system attempts to calculate the existing money supply and control by a complex detecting liabilities. With the separation into categories of M0 to M3, one tries to keep an overview. This can only be more rudimentary, because the largest part of the money now flows uncontrollably.

The human system does not need all this. The money here is quite simple, the amount of money. At any time, any central bank knows how much money is available and where it flows.

The amount of money varies in human monetary system by changing the number of inhabitants, by the changing economic output or by changing the base period. Thus, the central bank ensures that there is always enough money.

The central bank calculates monthly monetary quantity by multiplying the value with the human population. The difference from the previous month will be added or removed from the books of the central bank money buffer. This money will be destroyed or created. Depending on whether the human value was greater or smaller, or population more or less.

In addition, the central bank monitors the buffered money. At a certain lower limit of the base period is increased. From a certain upper limit of the base period will be reduced. This also makes money is destroyed or created.

The central banks have piled beside this buffer no more values. Neither gold nor currencies or securities.

However, the monthly adjusting the money supply is not stabilized prices. With the federal funds rate and the state interest and the base of purchasing power, the central bank has three tools with which they can effectively stabilize the prices.

3.5. Prime rate

The prime rate is a percentage of those at which banks can borrow money from the Central Bank. This will more or less expensive loans and interest income on savings is higher or lower. The central bank uses this instrument as well as in the past.

Banks, which have a license to borrow money from the central bank and may give this money to business or residential customers in the region, likewise, their loans granted must be available as capital at 100%. Thus, there is no private money creation more.

Increase loans, however, continue the money supply. Melts namely the money buffer of the central bank on a certain lower limit, they must increase the base period. Then, the value increases, which in turn increases the money supply. Conversely, this happens if the return to National Bank is greater than the outflow by borrowing.

3.6. State interest

The state rate is that rate at which the administrations of government, states, counties and municipalities may borrow money from the Central Bank. In human monetary system, these institutions can finance solely through the Central Bank. The state interest should be possible at the prime rate. Whereas common rules for changing the state interest rate be set before the introduction of the new system. As these rules look like in detail, is not so important, they just need to be the same for all.

The state interest is a further adjustment for the National Bank. Normally, the interest rate and the state interest should be the same. In an emergency, but can also be deviated from.

3.7. Base purchasing power

The base purchasing power is the most important element of human monetary system. It is a percentage of , human value, mixed with a percentage of median income. The central bank thereby engages by changing the formula. This formula should be optimized more and more over time, so that manual intervention is always less necessary.

> Example formula:
>
> (Human value x 0,0001 + Median) x 0,2 = Base purchasing power
>
> 90.000.000 x 0,0001 = (1900 + 1800) x 0,2 = € 740.--

The base purchasing power consists of a direct payment from the government to its citizens. For politicians, it is a social instrument to the guaranteed minimum income. For the central bank, it is an important tool to keep prices stable.

Technically, it is irrelevant who is entitled to this payment. It is important that the central bank is able to pump money into the market. It must be ensured that this money is consumed immediately, for only thus the purchasing power increases rapidly. Anyone who has no income receives the basic purchasing power, parents also for their children under 14 years.

The base purchasing power also determines the minimum wage. This is calculated from the base purchasing power multiplied by the factor 1.8. That is, the minimum wage is always higher by 80% than the direct payment of the state. It is important also to divide this month accompanied by the applicable standard working time. The resulting wage per hour may also not be exceeded. In a basic purchasing power of € 800, the minimum monthly salary € 1440 or the minimum hourly rate € 9 would be.

All wages above the minimum wage are only open to negotiation with the social partners.

Because of the constant comparison with other regions, an ideal formula is quickly found, with the base purchasing power is calculated.

Since the base purchasing power is also a percentage of the , human value, the specific amount of base purchasing power grows as increases GDP. This is an automatism which converts a part of the new economic growth in purchasing power.

Will be paid the basic purchasing power by the state. It is financed by the tax revenue of the state.

The base purchasing power is also the basis for an allowance. Over this allowance inheritance tax is payable. **Base purchasing power x base period** gives the amount above which inheritance tax (**base period / 10**) is due. For example:

Base purchasing power: € 800.--

Basis period: 300 years

| 800 x 300 = 240.000 Euro | 300 / 10 = 30 % |

Amounts under € 240,000 is tax free, over 30% inheritance tax due. There should be no exceptions. Reduce donations before death the allowance.

We can also agree on other numbers and formulas before the introduction of the system, which does not harm the entire system. The invoice must be the same for all participating regions. It is only important that the upper layer is forced to an interest in a harmonic function of the monetary system.

3.8. Social system

The reforms of the economy and the tax also will pave the way for a fundamental reform of the welfare system.

After the two reforms are carried out, many social achievements are superfluous.

In the Human monetary system wealthy and elderly people live mainly from their dividends. These dividends they receive through their ownership of shares in the economy.

Young people without inherited wealth live mainly of an unconditional basic income, which consists of the basic purchasing power and a few hours of work per week. They focus primarily on their education and the upbringing of their children.

This is not a paradise, because the basis of purchasing power decreases immediately when insufficient manpower available.

In the Human System labour income is subsidized below the minimum wage. Young people with no unearned income will therefore endeavour, as long as possible to take advantage of this subsidy.

Only when the unearned income has reached a certain level, the desire turns. Then, no longer yields the basis of purchasing power and the compensatory payment. Then it is worthwhile to massive savings, so you get more and more dividends from SSC shares.

Thus, each determined even when he wants to retire. Those who are not SSC shares save up to live in the age of the base of purchasing power.

Any citizen with primary residence in the national economy is automatically sickness, accident and nursing insurance. This state system is fully financed by taxes. Is billed with inclusion of the beneficiary. There is no power without a deductible.

The deductible prevents the ill-use of services of public health systems. Therefore, such deductibles must be appropriate to the income. The higher the income, the higher the deductible.

3.9. Basket of goods

The basket of products and services is very essential for the human benefit system. The decision on the contents of this basket of goods is an important task of central banks. Control and participation of parent institutions is important. Permanent transparency and accountability are fundamental condition.

The basket and the calculation of the tax rate on inheritances are the variables which must be the same for all participants in the human monetary system. But the VAT should be harmonized as possible, but this is not a condition.

3.10. Central Bank

The pivotal point in human Monetary System is the Central Bank. Private investments in a central bank, there is no longer.

The central task of this institution is to keep the inflation rate at 0%. The fluctuations are shifting from the prices on the human value.

Even when prices changes occur which are not always clear, the central bank has always been to keep the full control of the money supply, purchasing power and interest rates, the power prices stable.

As in the past, there will be a deflation in technical products. This is also exactly as before, to technical developments.

Climb or descent prices, the central bank react to a change in the prime rate, the base purchasing power or the state interest.

Before the introduction of the new monetary system also need to define rules that will later is improved. Rules that determine when, what measures are to be set. Under what conditions, either way needs to be responded. This is important so that all future central banks follow a line and always choose the most successful solution.

The long term, those regions are the most successful are those that have a balance between promotions of the lower layers, and strain the upper layers.

A bad policy always shows itself in human monetary system by increasing the inheritance tax. In most cases, bad policy is based on corruption. Therefore, the amount of this tax will in future be an indicator of corruption. For the first time humanity has at its disposal a system that restricts the corruption by an automatism.

In the human system, the money Statistical Office, the Treasury and the Central Bank must work closely together. A modern control by the Court of Auditors is absolutely necessary. Any decision is made only on the basis of statistical calculations and must be comprehensible for everyone. Lonely arbitrariness by a Fed chairman, there are no longer.

In addition to review by the Court of Auditors also a higher-level institution must perform tasks. This institution has in the human currency system in addition to controlling also sanction competence. Operates a regional central bank with false figures, this institution has immediate correction skills. Institutions, such as the World Bank or ECB get a significantly different task.

3.11. Trade Balance and Foreign Exchange

Foreign exchange accounts, there is no more money in the human system. Everything about money a region located in this region.

This results in an additional task for the central banks. The monetary compensation. To this end, each central bank has an account with all the other central banks. This can act citizens of different regions with each other. This is done automatically, without time delay and charging fees as long as the balance of trade is balanced.

In case of strong differences in trade balances it comes to disabilities. These disabilities are quite desired. Trade balances should, within certain limits, is compensated. It is the task of politics to prevent such disabilities by agreeing intergovernmental counter transactions and contracts.

For our modern technology, these networking and automatic postings is not a problem. This power of the central banks is taken for granted, such as the structure of the road network.

The huge market of forex trading comes to a complete standstill in the final.

3.12. Paper money and coins
Even in the old system, there are only 3% to 5% of the total amount of money than paper or coins. This does not change in the human system considerably.

Because of the steadily improving conditions for counterfeiters, the cashless monetary transactions should, as already previously to be further promoted. The validity of bills should not exceed 10 years. New certificates should be replaced every 5 to 8 years old. Each region can use their own bills or shared with other regions bills. Since the currencies no longer fluctuate, it is immaterial which currency is used.

Use more than one region, the same bills so a higher-level central bank is necessary. This would be the ECB in the European Union.

Each region can, however, use your own bills, money in the human system, this is not essential.

The coinage system should not be changed.

3.13. The conversion

Even before the first measure, extensive negotiations are required. The future program must set all system conditions. If an agreement is likely, the financial sector will reduce about 25% of its staff in the participating states. The reason is the changes to be expected. However, the Financial Market Authority and the Banking Supervision will require most of these people. The work of these two institutions is to change, and in the first years thereafter, a considerable rise.

A decision by the European Union, the changeover to the human system can be preceded only an extensive replacement of the top positions at the national and international level. One may in this respect have no illusions. At present all the important positions are held by people who have no interest in a humane solution. On the contrary, on the levers of power sit especially those with a close relationship to institutions that triggered the recent crisis, or at least benefited from it, have. By focusing on the Group "Goldman Sachs" However, it is easy to identify these persons.

At least one year before the changeover should the economy be reformed through the introduction of SSC.

The first measure is to collect all loans and other contracts that create money, as well as in the establishment of buffer account and all other relevant accounts with the central bank. The banks would begin repayment to the Central Bank.

The second measure is the rescheduling of all sovereign debt in the financial market by the central bank and the beginning of the repayment by the central bank. These contrasts with accounts of the administration of government, states and municipalities, there flow all future repayments from these institutions. At the same time the sale of all the reserves of the central bank is done. Gold is through this step, a metal, like any other. The gold price is already falling massively.

The third measure is the establishment of mechanisms the base purchasing power. Pension benefits are paid out early and resolved the pension and health insurance, or incorporated into the ministries. Payments for pensions, health care, social assistance and est. are replaced with the base purchasing power. Pensioners of the future will live on their company shares and / or the base purchasing power. Also living children and young people and those adults who can not manage to generate enough income of their own mainly by base purchasing power. In the distant future, there will be very few people who have not lived sometime during their lives from the base purchasing power, which is a matter of course.

If the euro area converted to the human money, so he is already after a short time the reserve currency, because by stable prices, all other economies forced to devalue against the euro.

At first attacks of the globalized powers can only be fought with strong mechanisms. These include social duties, environmental taxes and targeted policy. Although to some international agreements must be terminated.

Because of the horrendous national debt of most countries, very high base periods are initially necessary. This results in the most indebted regions to inheritance taxes of over 90%. Only the tax-free allowances can be inherited. This fact is the great obstacle for this system, because the ruling upper classes to defend their property by any means. However, this fact also bestows an advantage. This benefit is an additional control element for the central bank. Due to the enormous revenue from the inheritance tax, they can repay debt faster than agreed. You can control, that is, slow down or speed up this process thus, depending on the need.

Many banks will go bankrupt because they have to capitalize on their loans and contracts to 100% for the conversion. These will be sadly many. Therefore we need before the conversion a functioning liquidation procedure for banks. Most such banks be nationalized, however, converted into a SSC and sold again. Savings have to be secured by government institutions. The great advantage of this process is the disappearance of virtual assets, translucency, which consist only of artificial inventions of securities departments of banks. This process can shrink the entire money supply and thereby the initial high base periods can be shortened.

Financial, insurance and gambling companies are all converted into a SSC.

The larger states should consider whether it is not better to install two or more central banks. The regions should consistently have a roughly equal economic strength. It is much more useful if economically weak regions install their own central bank, the human value can depreciate against the stronger region. The division of the national debt must be negotiated in this case before.

Along with the change needs to be improved and harmonized the political system.

In addition to the primary task of the Central Bank, stable prices, there is always pressure to reduce the inheritance tax. For this purpose, the region must reduce the base period. However this only works if either the human value increases, or the entire money supply is reduced.

The money supply to reduce means a contraction of the economy. In contrast to the current system, this may well be a viable option in human monetary system. For example, if the population is continuously supplied with a new technology, it takes much less resources to get the technique upright.

The human value increases when the productivity increases. That is, in this region it is possible to produce the same amount of goods and services with less effort. The human value of the money supply increases. So you can reduce the base period, which makes the money supply shrink back to the previous level and lowers the inheritance tax. However, there are also efforts to the contrary. The lower the inheritance tax is, the lower is also the tax-free allowance, so that the taxable section of the population is growing. This creates a political counter-pressure, which aims to increase the inheritance tax.

The debts of the administrations of State; countries and communities do no more harm. These debts increase while the quantity of money, but its reduction is not harmful. Although constantly rising debt hurt no longer the currency of society but. Because of the high repayments, taxes are getting higher. In the long run only reduce the debt or at least stop the debt is a solution. The debt, taxes and services of the state should have in the long run a harmonious relationship to each other as possible.

In the longer term there is a traveling movement to regions with low base periods, because there you can bequeath to his children his assets cheaper. This influx forces mostly to an increase in the base period. This again causes the opposite.

After a few years the human monetary system is a matter of course. The new generations can not make a real picture is from the old injustices.

Example Albania

This example is intended to show how a small country like Albania, surrounded on the human monetary system.

First, politicians are establishing themselves in one or more parties in the Albanian parliament. They are referred to as "Median".

The Median should have about 10% of seats in Parliament at first decisions in their direction to obtain.

Initially, they are naturally strong hostility. They tried to vilify, it is denoted as the left anarchists and the like. On the other hand, they are berated as a right neoliberals, because they threaten many social achievements.

It is because of this contradiction, many young Albanians will watch the new system even more accurately and many of which are new media leaders, when they begin to understand the system.

First, the media agents succeed enforce in Parliament the introduction of the new form of society SSC. This seems also many other politicians as desirable and they get a majority for the SSC.

The Median meticulously paying attention to the fact that transparency is introduced in the economics ministry, so that corruption in the new market does not get any opportunity. There are well-trained engineers and computer scientists in their ranks, so a fantastic example system is created.

Many young entrepreneurs take advantage of the new opportunities and make their company around. Many to save taxes, but most of them to new capital to get through new issues. Many new companies start using the new exchange. Even abroad Albanians around the world observe the development in the home and start SSC to acquire shares.

The Median increase in the next election their seats and come as a coalition partner in the government. You will receive the Ministry of Economy and improve the system so that their electoral system is also useful for political elections.

The first local elections be carried out successfully with the new system. The world press begins to be interested in the events in Albania.

In the next elections, the Median obtain a majority in Parliament and decide first a comprehensive tax reform.

After that, they can also introduce the human monetary system.

The money supply in Albania compared to other European incredibly low.

The Albanian Statistical Office, together with the Ministry of Finance and the Central Bank to determine the definition of the basis period for the start of the new system.

One must decide between the initial monetary stability and the resulting estate tax there. If small inheritances are tax exempt, the base period must be as high as possible. If the currency remain stable vis, must the money supply, and thus the base period, be as small as possible.

They agree for example to a base period of 162 years. The Lek is characterized initially lose some, stable prices the same but soon again. This results in the following figures.

Population: 3.150.143
GDP per capita: 431.747 ALL 3.086 €
Base Period: 162 years
Human value: 69.947.235 ALL 499.932 €
Money supply: 220.343.795.483.030 ALL
        1.574.857.290.276 €

Base purchasing power: 15.614 ALL   87 €
Minimum wage: 21.826 ALL   156 €
Median: 25.604 ALL   183 €
Inheritance from: 2.538.590 ALL   18.144 €
Inheritance Tax: 16.2%   (inheritances under 2.538.590 ALL are tax free)

After the conversion, the numbers change continuously, because the purchasing power is steadily increasing. After 10 years of stable Lek is the hardest currency. Albania is called the Switzerland in the south. It has been aligned with the standard of living of the euro zone. Because of the high amounts in Lek Albania leads after 13 years of the euro.

3.14. Differences and similarities
If you look at both systems exactly the differences are not as great as it seems.

The difference is only in the controllability and the control options.

Similar to the creation of money the old system, the money supply also increases when the demand for loans increases. The difference lies in the automatic mechanisms that ensure transparency and security.

The uncontrollable global money market is broken down into manageable and above all controllable units. Global trade is hardly changed. The financial sector is again an auxiliary tool of the real economy. In the old system was from the financial industry an own industry with their own products. This is also the big difference. Both financial and insurance industry will return to service industries. These produce no more products.

The biggest difference, however, under the direct influence of the central bank to lower incomes. Only this action makes the system more crisis-proof and effective.

In addition, the policy is required to redistribute the work as possible to the entire population. It is not advisable to leave this to the social partners, for business ways of thinking can cause considerable damage to these sensitive areas. If productivity is growing faster than the demand for goods, the work is less. This process sets up the new system at no more damage. In the old system, this process is a disaster. It is the beginning of the end.

Paying attention to price differences there will be as before. The price wars of trade, there will be more. Central banks try to gather the medium-term and long-term price shifts to compensate. Thus, all current leading products in the areas of food, clothing, housing and est. remain, on average, over the years, always the same.

The human system represents money with very little effort getting the optimal amount of money available. Stupidity and criminality can not harm the system. Due to the rapid control of purchasing power and interest rates, the system is completely resistant to the crisis and no longer dependent on growth of the economy.

The modern skills available in the old system exclusively in the service of profit. In the human system, these skills will be used to install permanent natural order and peace without the pursuit of profit maximization to reduce.

3.15. Summary

In human currency system, all regions have their own central bank and a certain amount of money that is shown on the accounts of the Central Bank.

Money a region will no longer remove the region. Cash flows over the regions also always lead through the Central Bank. These postings are carried out without delay and are free of charge.

The base period of a region, multiplied by the GDP / per capita gives the human value. The human value of a region, multiplied by the population gives the money supply of a region.

Human value = GDP/capita x Base period
Money supply = Human value x population

In the human system, the currency price fluctuations shift to the human value. The prices for all basic needs remain the same over long periods. This simplifies the entire economic life considerably.

The most important value in human monetary system is the base purchasing power, which is paid out to citizens as guaranteed minimum income from the state. The amount of payment varies by the work of the Central Bank. She holds it, together with the interest rate prices stable. The central bank sets the height of the base purchasing power is not directly fixed, but changed and improved a mathematical formula.

Example formula:
(Human value x 0.0001 + median) x 0.2 = basic purchasing power

The central bank is calculated on a monthly basis, the money supply and compares the result with the previous month. This money will be destroyed or created.

Depending on whether GDP was greater than or less than or residents were more or less.

In addition, the central bank monitors the buffered money at the central bank. At a certain lower limit of the base period is increased. From a certain upper limit of the base period will be reduced. This also makes money is destroyed or created. This also affects the modalities of the inheritance tax.

The money in the market, and therefore prices, the central bank regulated by changing the base purchasing power and interest rates. The policy contributes with its tax policies also share in these tasks.

The height of the base period determined the inheritance tax rate. As well as, together with the base purchasing power over the free allowance will be payable on the inheritance tax. Reduce donations before the death of the allowance.

base period / 10 = Inheritance tax
e.g. 300years/10 = 30%
base purchasing power x base period = allowance
e.g. 800€ x 300years = 240.000€

The height of the base purchasing power determines the minimum wage in the region.

Minimum wage = basic purchasing power x 1.8
e.g. € 720.00 x 1.8 = € 1296.00 - = € 8.10 / hour

Central banks hoard no values, with the exception of the money supply buffer. Gold is a metal in the human system, like any other.

The FMA (Financial Market Supervision) ensures that no money is created by private and other institutions.

This task is enormous, as it seems. Money is in the new system a service of the state. Private money may no longer exist therefore. This also applies to all swap transactions. There are on the financial markets, various forms of private money.

4. General thoughts

4.1. Compulsory education
Very old is compulsory for male members of the Jewish religion. It is the only religion was the reading of the traditional records for large parts of the male population duty. Although Christianity and Islam have the same roots, this custom has not there enforced to the extent.

It was not until the Reformation, initiated by Martin Luther, caused the first attempts to introduce a compulsory education. Especially Catholic ruling houses were often strongly opposed to any compulsory education. There were several reasons for it certainly. A very banal reason was the need of children for work, especially in agriculture. However, the more important reason was the fear of their own subjects. If the lower layers were beginning to understand the Bible and other works, it could push doubts about the political system arise. These concerns were proven justified, as school education and the French Revolution are in a close connection.

In the Austrian Habsburg Empire from Maria Theresa, compulsory education was then more of a protection against unbridled education. The children referred to the authorities began to manipulate. Accordingly, the form and content of education was established. Unfortunately, we find in the modern system still elements of these forms. Just as bad, the military was embossed by the Prussian in the German Kingdom. These elements can still be found in the modern school system.

As a conclusion we can state that the compulsory education has hardly humanitarian roots and the formation of the lower stratum of the population is not a pressing concern of the upper class. To date, there are currents that prevent educational reforms for exactly this reason.

4.2. School system

Man has by itself a natural need to research and discover. Any coercion is already a failure of the system. When children experience security and love, explore on their own the entire environment. Every school system that makes use of this phenomenon is suitable. The creation of fear and coercion, however, causes the exact opposite. The natural tendency is damaged so that the first steps for underage citizens are done with it.

The appropriate early childhood education is mainly due to the Hungarian paediatrician Emmi Pikler. Their methods are derived from the works of Elsa Gindler and

Heinrich Jacoby. Since Pikler there are many advancements, many are good, some developments are more likely to regress again. The reason for this is usually the delusional power in our society.

Even in the normal education, there are currents, which take into account the above facts. However, they are now in the minority. They are based on Heinrich Pestalozzi and Maria Montessori. The best free Pedagogy of Rebecca Wild was realized in a private school in Ecuador. Graduates were not only well trained in this school, she attended this school with enthusiasm. They learned to put other people in a natural way limits, so they were very suitable for leadership positions in business. Unfortunately, this school was closed several years ago.

However, there are other flows with satisfactory results. When students go willingly and voluntarily in the school and comparative studies show a satisfactory result, then a school system is good, as long as it is also the financial needs on average. Hate the children to school, comparative studies, the financial requirements are unsatisfactory or too high, school systems are bad.

The most negative, however, the modern high schools. They work almost exclusively with fear and hidden constraints and bring almost only immature people out. Reviews by students through adults are more meaningful, the younger the children. Students are motivated by older students need something less. Adults no longer review. However, there is in our universities a span assessment; the majority of students just want a good report or an academic title. Pure study interests you meet only in exceptional cases.

An important political act of the future would be the abolition of titles and reviews, from the testimony to the Nobel Prize. Reviews of adults by adults represents an unworthy reduction, it should be not forbidden, however, constitute a violation of taboo.

To avoid misunderstandings, the listing of completed performance is not a review. Resumes are quite sufficient for entry into the industry and the career development is not required of these reviews. The performance of each people expresses itself all by itself; in any industry everyone knows the best, even without a title.

Certain knowledge of the rules are the first-run of activities necessary this knowledge you can easily query nowadays with computer programs, it also needs doing any assessment by humans. The presence of necessary experience obtained by documenting processes. The standardized documentation replaced in the distant future today certificates and titles.

4.3. Television

The teacher Rebecca Wild leads the television on in a list of active threats. In the educational environment of children no active threats may be present. This is a prerequisite in order to be made up of children, free and independent people.

The danger posed by television, is in addiction and in the intention to manipulate the operator. This risk is not limited to children. Only a careful handling of this medium can minimize this risk.

However, a complete renunciation of television is not necessary. The reversal of the program design is essential, however. The television program one can also make yourself. Targeted selection and programmed recording of desired programs in reducing the risk. If one does not generally to series, so you have already taken the most important step. One should be consistent, because the propaganda industry produces nowadays for every imaginable taste a television series, so almost anyone can fall into this trap.

The most harmful effect of television is simply the harvesting of life. This also applies to popular documentaries. Their indiscriminate consumption only costs a lot of time and leads to no real education. Here, the only time dislocation, one sees such records on only when you want to study this issue themselves.

If you want to do without television, so is an easy-to-program hard disk recorder the best means to make his own program. The track messages and the consumption of good movies part of many people today simply to contrast and nothing is wrong with that.

Politically public service broadcasting should be separated from the advertising industry. The dependence of the advertising industry and the worldwide agencies should be as low as possible. Of this, however, we are far away. The trend is exactly the other way. For today, public service broadcasters, the charges are not justified.

4.4. Health
Studying medicine or someone like to make later career in the private sector, he begins after graduation in the public sector. The Ministry of Health with tasks such as food inspection, approval of drugs and chemicals for the food industry, setting tolerable limits of harmful substances and the like are his orders. Almost all medical studies are done in partnership with industry and financed by it.

This is for a limited number of people. The industry is looking away from the pool those people out, which are suitable for high-paying positions in the companies in question. After a few years, everyone has established contacts and networks that are useful in his career.

This brief description of the state of our health workforce policies makes quite clear why all decisions are made in this area, not in the ministry, but in the boardrooms of corporations.

4.4.1. Vaccinations

There is a large amount of studies on the consequences and benefits of vaccination. There are also plenty of books about the topic.

But one thing is very striking. Harmful vaccinations are precisely those in which the active ingredient amplifier, called adjuvants, consist of aluminium compounds.

Sometimes you can hardly understand why recognized health experts located so little from prohibiting such substances at last. It almost seems as if there is a global non-disclosure agreement in the industry.

The Danish physician Peter Aaby has created the best studies on this topic. He and his wife have been working in the African Guinea-Bissau; they have explored the relationship between child mortality and vaccination.

The huge flooding of counter studies were funded by the pharmaceutical industry or at least distorted by corrupt experts.

The lack of propriety can be seen from the name of the so-called "ethics committees" of the medical universities. While this is not to say all members of these commissions are corrupt, the present condition has little in common with ethics, however.

I can only advise anyone who educates young children, to learn exactly.

4.4.2. Aluminium

The metal aluminium was classified as harmless 100 years. Well, it turns out suddenly; it is much more dangerous than other metals, such as lead or mercury.

Again, I can only advise everyone to inform themselves, because aluminum acts slowly and damages the body slowly. The most common disease that their occurrence aluminum compounds are involved, the dementia disease, "Alzheimer's".

Not only in vaccinations, aluminum is used. It is located in suntan lotion, cosmetics, medicines, in foods, it is used for drinking water treatment and more.

With this wide range of applications, it no longer seems surprising why those diseases increase greatly in which aluminum supposedly plays a role.

The researcher "**Christopher Exley**" mentions the following diseases whose development is causally involved aluminium. He indicates a likelihood value of 1 through 10.

Alzheimer	7-8
Parkinson	4-6
Dialyse-Demenz	10
Multiple Sklerose	4-6
Epilepsie	7-8
Osteomalacie	10
Osteoporose	4-6
Arthritis	5-7
Anämie	10
Asthma	7-9
MMF (Makrophagische Myofascitis)	8-10
Occurring after vaccination hyper-	8-10

sensitivity to aluminum
Morbus Chron 7-9
Sarkoidose 7-9

What can you do as a layman?

First of all, inform. The medical journalist "**Bert Ehgartner**" has already published two books on this issue.

Where are containing these compounds? Nothing to buy, where aluminum is contained more. Beware, there are even regular table salt with this poison. It is used to make the salt more trickles. The same is unfortunately also often made with milk powder in coffee machines.

Here is a list of cosmetic products with aluminum compounds:
Linden Voss Tripl Dry
Yves Rocher Transat
Jafra Gently Effective Anti-Perspirant
Nivea Double effect
Hydrofugal Sensitive Stick
Rexona Woman Cotton Dry Stick
Dove Christal Deodorant
Maria Galland Cream Deodorant
Biotherm Deo Pure
Pedibaer Fußdeospray
Beiersdorf Hidro fugal
Spirig Hautschutzcreme
Vichy Deodorant-Creme
Fa Deodorant
Bac Aloe Vera Sensitive
Dove Deo-Spray
Nivea Creme
Just Natural Deo Edelweiss
Dr. Grandel Eye Care Contour Creme
Korres Thymianhonig Gesichtscreme
Rugard Vitamin Cream
Carita International Teint Lissant

Dermalogica Ultra Sensitive faceblock spf25
Roche-Posay Anthelios LSF20
L'Oreal Solar Expertise Aktiv LSF 50+
Vichy Make Up Flüssig
babylove Sonnenmilch
Babor Body Line Thermal Body Lotion
Weleda Iris Feuchtigkeitscreme
Couleur Caramel Eyeliner
Joop Velvet Body Lotion
AOK Thermo-Aktiv Maske
Oil of Olaz Aktivschutz Fluid für reife Haut
Guinot Creme Hydrallergic
medipharma cosmetics Olivenöl Gesichtspflege
Ellen Betrix Soft Resistannce Make up
Garnier Apres Pflegende Feuchtigkeitsmilch
Nu Skin Sunright Body Block 30
Dr. Armah-Biomedica La Volta Shea Sun Lotio LSF25 Wasserfest
Cos Line GmbH cl Deo-Kristall Mineral Spray
Dr. Baumann Lippenstift Nr. 7421-7449
Dr. Baumann Deo mild und Deo extra mild

Another important step would be to draw in his circle of awareness on the subject. The cosmetics industry is already responding, it is even advertised as "aluminum-free".

Now a list of e-number with aluminum in our foods.

E127 erythrosine aluminum lake

is used for coloring of red cherries, because the dye does not pass into the juice. Also in drugs and cosmetics in use. (for example, red lipstick)

E132 Indicarmin aluminum dye

Green, violet, brown in confectionery, pastries, liqueurs, ice cream, desserts. Color of drugs and cosmetics.

E173 aluminum

silver-gray dye for confectionery, liquorice dragees, decorations on cookies and cakes. Also for medicines and cosmetics.

E520 Aluminium sulphate

E522 AluminiumKaliSulfat

E523 Aluminium ammonium sulphate

Stabilizers, pickled fruit is al dente, sausage casings made of natural casings are fixed.

E541 Treat Sodium aluminum phosphate

Baking biscuit biscuits.

E554 Sodium aluminum silicate

E555 Potassium aluminum silicate

E556 Calcium aluminum silicate

E559 Aluminium silicate

These silicates increase the flowability of powder products, as well as the bonding of slice of cheese.

E1452 AluminiumOckenylSuccinat

Prevents clots in many products.

It is only to be hoped that our health policy makers finally wake up from their lethargy.

One thing you can say this with certainty. The global aluminum industry has a lot of power and exercises it too, or would already have something done.

4.4.3. Plastics

Similar to the aluminum is true for plastics. Many substances in these products are harmful to health. Especially the plasticizers of PVC provide a serious problem for a are also called phthalates and intervene directly in the hormonal balance of living organisms. Even the smallest amount of damage the hormone control, so in this area have limits no sense. In Europe, they are indeed used little more, but by importing from Asia reaches a lot of this poison to us.

Only a ban on these substances makes sense. Please get informed.

4.4.4. Teflon

The third scandalous poison is in teflon-coated cookware. The poison is actually called polytetrafluoroethylene. Teflon is a brand name of the company DuPont.

From about 235 ° C. Such dishes poisons begins to secrete substances. The poison fluoropolymer is specified as the most toxic, it can even be fatal.

These things are not contrived about the hair. The company DuPont would not have $ 16.5 million compensation in 2005 paid if he had not done any damage. It related to studies on Perflouroktanacid (PFOA). DuPont had the study kept secret, although it proves the health hazards of PFOA.

The U.S. Environmental Protection Agency (EPA): *PFOA is toxic and carcinogenic, it accumulates in the body, can lead to infertility, when heated, forms toxic gases and in the manufacture of PFOA into waste wa-*

ter, where it is no longer degradable. PFOA is used inter alia for the production of Teflon.

4.5. Leisure

In order to make the people's leisure most of the money is used worldwide. Nothing could be more dangerous than when 50% of voters leisure would make even in a democracy. You pay athletes, actors and other celebrities the highest sums to avert this danger. And this with resounding success.

High jugglers, from antiquity to today, a must live for all time.

4.5.1. Cabaret und Comedy

Due to the current popularity of the cabaret scene, it is worthwhile to invest some thought into this profession. As with all topics, helps to look into the story to come to a deeper understanding.

A circumstance that immediately catches the eye, it quickly becomes apparent. The greater the dissatisfaction with the government, the higher the interest in the satirical view of politics and its actors. The psychological function of this fact probably lies in a valve. This valve acts as well as the tradition of the carnival. The anger at political problems becomes more bearable. The process of "making ridiculous" the ruler gives temporary relief.

Conversely, this valve has long been used by those in power to stay in power. Or in other words, to keep the suppression at a high level.

Historically, this can be observed especially in the Roman Empire. The festival of Saturnalia, in which class differences were eliminated, was with increasing problems getting longer and eventually took over a week. The slaves were served by their masters at this time to the amusement of the participants.

The court jester at all European courts met later the same purpose. And the carnival is nothing more than the continuation of the Roman Saturnalia. Our comedians are therefore nothing more than the court jesters of the Middle Ages.

Derived from these findings, it seems not so surprising when you look at the income of today's comedians. The well-known by television comedian in the German-speaking area are consistently millionaires today. Even today's government knows why.

Looking at the cabaret scene from this angle, the incompatibility of satire and serious politics is obvious. Some of today's players this approach would certainly do well.

4.6. Nuclear energy

When it comes to nuclear energy, I would like to express my rejection straight away. The radioactive radiation is too dangerous, so I can use this form of energy not currently advocate.

We do not have to decide whether we use this form of energy or not, for the earth is already full of nuclear power plants. It was and is a completely irresponsible decision because we are technically this is not developed enough.

I am concerned but especially to the disposal of the radiating waste which arises from the operation of such power stations. It is in fact meant in a totally wrong direction.

One seeks to store geological strata to secure the waste for decades. This one seems to actually believe that you could prevent contamination so for thousands of years.

The correct solution of the final nuclear waste storage, is exactly the opposite of a geologically safe storage. Not in quiet rock or salt formations of the waste should be stored, but in geologically active zones as possible. There, the waste should be introduced so that it hits as soon as possible on liquid magma of the Earth's interior. Thus, this material is once again completely neutralized and represents no danger to our descendants.

Geologists would have to clarify which method is best suited for this. Whether it is better to introduce the material into the lithosphere, where it penetrates through the plate tectonics of the earth over the asthenosphere magma into the mesosphere, or whether the material is introduced directly into volcanic magma. Open magma sources, there are supposedly only five in the world.

As a layman, I would prefer the second option. Reminds me of the Ethiopian Erta Ale comes in the East African grave breach in mind.

Europe, and especially Germany, should generally have a little bit more courage when it comes to such research. Initiatives may also arise from the policy. You do not always wait for research and industry. Finally, here diplomatic agreements are necessary. In addition, cooperation with the Ethiopian military is necessary if you want to restart attempts Castor containers to throw off from aircraft and to spend at high speed in the liquid magma.

4.7. Energy transition

There are a number of fatal errors, not only in the energy transition, but also in the entire energy policy. As so often these days, we see here, as in particular the interests of large corporations are realized; citizens' interests are in second place.

The barely-thought-problems are the various networks. This issue affects other areas such as communication, shipping, water supply and waste management. Most importantly is electricity and gas. Even before privatization independent studies would have been necessary. Meanwhile, the policy has been so corrupted, so that truly independent studies are scarcely feasible.

You can still think about the best solution, however. It's all about meaning. Can it really make sense to run multiple networks simultaneously in the same room? These parallel operations there in telephone, postal and parcel service. Give independent calculations that it makes more sense not to fight a competing parallel operation, as well as the whereabouts of such networks in the private ownership must be reconsidered. In any case, you need control authorities, which provide cost honesty, when there is no pressure on costs is through competition.

Where competition is wanted is a feed-in tariff, as it currently exists in the current alternative energy, pure poison. If the government wants to promote alternative energy, so he should do this in investments, but in no case the product, which is regulated by price competition. Solar panels should be encouraged, for example, the roof installation to the extent that it pays for homeowners. Same time, this promotion may not be too high, the resulting installation companies should have a long-term stock.

4.8. Slavery

The lack of freedom of people, there are probably as long as there are people.

This is, however, about seeing the word itself more closely. For several years, this home is as good as undisputed. Contrary to all previous assumptions, the truth probably has at last prevailed on the origin of the word.

In the first millennium every people called the enslaved people to the peoples names, from which came most of the oppressed. In the Roman Empire, these were the Slavic peoples. The name "slave" therefore means nothing more than "Slav". This roman name later continued by the world.

Why not long ago carried consequences from this realization is not only a mystery to me. In today's sensitivity with all terms that have even remotely to do with racism, the fact is all the more inexplicable.

We also hear much of the Slavic peoples themselves should in fact a cry be heard by the Slavic world, where this fact is probably still displaced.

If someone other rebukes when they describe dark-skinned people as Negroes, as he is to clarify the origin of the word "slave" once. In Europe, the word "negro" never had a negative or racist meaning, but the word "slave"?

It would be highly straighten at the time this linguistic derailment. The word "slave," "slavery," etc. should as soon as possible its place among the inappropriate, racist expressions are taking. The ban should, in my opinion, getting the first place among all racist expressions.

5. Philosophical thoughts

The overload of information makes students often historians who gather all the past about a topic. To develop your own ideas, hardly have time. The philosophy of this applies to an even greater extent than the economics.

Historians of philosophy, therefore, there is in abundance. In most cases, they are satisfied if they have already established itself as a title and a body recognized in society.

If one has to study a genuine interest in the sense of being, so you need abbreviations. Ways to avoid the abundance of information. These lines provide the interested parties with an opportunity to do so.

Make sure to read the books " The Spell of the Sensuous " by David Abram, " Jenseits von begabt und unbegabt " by Heinrich Jacoby.

This proposal I do not because I think these books for the source of all truths, but because they illustrate something very important. With the help of these books you can not only understand the distinction between mind and spirit, but you get a chance to experience this directly.

It makes no sense to study philosophy, if one equates his **mind** with his **spirit**.

The mind is only a tool of the spirit. He stands about as to the spirit, as the **shadow** to the **light**.

It is not enough just to know this, you must fully internalize. As the consciousness of modern man is a long time in the field of the mind, one can also speak of a necessary humility. This humility is necessary to operate philosophy makes sense.

The next step is the study of the discoveries of quantum physics. This is important because this science has encountered a limit. This limit is very similar to the boundary between mind and spirit.

For a long time, there are terms such as "microcosm" and "macrocosm." They come from old theories that assume a solar system would be equal to an atom. It was assumed that still exist a small world in each world. All these theories are refuted today.

There are also modern theories such as "chaos theory", the theory of "parallel universe" or "multiverse". These theories are similar and, in my opinion, most of the time all evil. They all come from ignorance of the border between spirit and understanding.

In addition to quantum physics, one should also note the astrophysics. In particular, the research on "anti-matter" and "black holes" are interesting for the philosopher. For even these show us the limits of our material world.

Now what is behind these limits? Quite simply, the metaphysics. The world outside of space and time. The Divine is a world in which there is neither space nor time. For the mind this world is a paradox, so he is not responsible for it. It is the world of the spirit that is at home there.

Actually, you know all this for a long time. This mystery is explained in detail in all religions and mythologies. The world of spirit is the Mythos. The world of the mind is the Logos. In the mythology but I will not go into in this book. However the limits of understanding.

Many questions were not more if you internalized the knowledge addressed.

"If man has an immortal spirit?" Of course the spirit is immortal, if he lives in a world in which there is no time.

"Is the universe infinite?" No. It always takes exactly one that place; it needs to solve the polar incompatibilities. Incompatibilities can not be resolved in the timelessness. Each pole needs its own time. The changing of the poles can be the voltage between the poles become smaller until they reunite and disappear out of time. Just observe the quantum physicist in their trials.

"Was there a Big Bang?" Yes, there is a constant, somewhere. Each was born in the time inconsistency is a big bang, some are large, some very small.

"Is there extraterrestrial life?" There is nothing in the universe other than life. There are only shapes that are not apparent to our minds as life. The life on earth is merely a form of infinitely many.

In addition to the terms "spirit" and "mind" there are many terms that are important for the philosopher.

The philosopher can not afford to integrate the understanding and reason in the term "**intelligence**" is. It is precisely this confusion leads to the large aberrations in the philosophical literature.

Intelligence is a Roman term. It simply means to read and select. It is the lowest form of acting. Even a machine is capable of. Each single-celled organisms in

145

nature can select materials that it needs. His intellect allows him to survive by recognizing harmful and useful selects. The intellect processed information from the sensors of the body in the brain. He can thus control body reactions directly, or by hormones produce **feelings** in the soul.

The spirit, however, produces **sensations**. He does not need to the brain. Sensation means "find themselves". This refers to our spirituality, the mind, to our sprit.

For our soul, it makes no difference whether there are feelings or sensations, they always respond with **emotions**.

We also have a function in the soul, which controls our emotions. **Reason**. On Reason have only living beings.

The reason adjusts the emotions to the environment. She works closely with the intellect, but does something else entirely. Feelings and sensations lead to emotions that arises by reason of it's **behavior**.

The **consciousness** of living beings is mostly in this function at home. Only man shifted his consciousness for a long time in the mind, very rarely also in the spirit.

All these are really issues of **psychology**. However, this young science does not know these differences. Therefore, it is also a world of illusions. From the self-deception to disappointment. Since its creation it has constantly changed. The most curious art concepts originate from psychology. The term "emotional intelligence" is one of them. That is why the philosopher should keep away from psychology as possible. He gets lost otherwise, like Hansel and Gretel fairy tale.

However, there is a world between reality and the world without time and space. Our physicists have come to the edge of the world. There is already the **polarity**, but no more **duality**.

Solid matter no longer exists there. In religions and mythologies often several layers of this world are described. For the philosopher is only important that time already has a quality there.

The quantity of time there but not in the form as we know it from the duality. Without duality two bodies can occupy the same space. Or, conversely, a body can be in two different places at the same time.

One could this world be called the "**generation**". Night after night we walk through this world in our dreams.

Creation arises when **generating** married to **reality**.

This other world is'd guess a lot more in this world than you. Our consciousness is only fractions of a second outside the present; it is in this in-between world.

Now we can ask ourselves questions.

"Is there also an immortal soul and rebirth?" There are in-between world of dead spirits. This term is used for people who have their spirit is completely unconscious. That's why sleep is often referred to as "the little death".

Look to one of the many "Zombie Movies" on. These are namely the parables of the intermediate world. Tried you doing to identify with the Zombie's. These are the ones where you tear off the head without hesitation. Then you know the importance of dead spirits in the intermediate world.

Only the higher layers of the soul those are reborn in a new form. If a person has no awareness in these areas, one can hardly speak of rebirth. Nothing of what is characterized these people born again.

"Is there time travel?" Yes, of course. We constantly undertake journeys into the future and into the past. The physical body is but trapped in the present. There is no way to change this.

All stories are just to allegories. All art is a manifestation of the intermediate world. Try the parables to conceive. One finds in modern art, movies, very often enigmatic parables that remain most hidden.

This applies to everything from the "Vampire". Or the area of "man and machine". Both consciously and unconsciously, many people have recognized the parable of the film "The Matrix." This is the true reason for the success of this work.

"What is the meaning of life?". No wonder the two words "**sence**" and "**being**" in some languages are pronounced in exactly the same. Being in the divine world, that is the meaning. As soon as one does not exist in complete love and harmony, creates a discrepancy. This is followed by a fall in the time.

There still remain infinitely many questions unanswered. The attempt to answer this, that's philosophy.

www.ingramcontent.com/pod-product-compliance
Lightning Source LLC
Chambersburg PA
CBHW030754180526
45163CB00003B/1014